AN ARRANGEMENT OF SKIN

ANNA JOURNEY

· · · · · · · · · ·

ESSAYS

COUNTERPOINT

BERKELEY

Library of Congress Cataloging-in-Publication Data is Available

Cover design by Kelly Winton
Cover Image: *The Penitent and the Patient*, 2009, by Ryan McLennan
30" x 52" acrylic and graphite on paper
Interior design by Tabitha Lahr

ISBN 978-1-61902-847-0

COUNTERPOINT
2560 Ninth Street, Suite 318
Berkeley, CA 94710
www.counterpointpress.com

Printed in the United States of America
Distributed by Publishers Group West

10 9 8 7 6 5 4 3 2 1

This book is a work of nonfiction. The names of several of the people and institutions
in it have been changed.

Beckian Fritz Goldberg, "Prologue as Part of the Body" from *Lie Awake Lake*.
Copyright ©2005 by Beckian Fritz Goldberg. Reprinted with the permission of
Oberlin College Press, www.oberlin.edu/ocpress.

Jack Gilbert, "Trying to Have Something Left Over" from *The Great Fires: Poems,
1982-1992*. Copyright © 1994 by Jack Gilbert. Reprinted with the permission of
Alfred A. Knopf, an imprint of the Knopf Doubleday Publishing Group, a division of
Penguin Random House LLC. All rights reserved.

for my parents: Cindy and Tim Journey

CONTENTS

. . . .

Acknowledgments / vii

An Arrangement of Skin   / 3

Birds 101   / 15

The Goliath Jazz / 33

Epithalamium with Skunk Pigs / 45

The Guineveres / 59

Strange Merchants / 81

Little Face / 93

A Flicker of Animal, a Flank / 107

Pangaea for Alice / 113

A Common Skin / 125

Prologue as Part of the Body / 135

Retro Anatomy of a String Bass / 157

Modifying the Badger / 169

Bluebeard's Closet / 181

ACKNOWLEDGMENTS

I'm grateful to the editors and staff of the following publications in which these essays appeared, sometimes in different form: *AGNI*: "A Common Skin," "A Flicker of Animal, a Flank," "An Arrangement of Skin," and "Little Face"; *At Length*: "Strange Merchants"; *Blackbird*: "Bluebeard's Closet"; *Catapult*: "Birds 101"; *diode*: "Epithalamium with Skunk Pigs" (as "A Strange Conjunction"); *Poetry Daily* Prose Feature: "Modifying the Badger" (reprint); *Prairie Schooner*: "The Goliath Jazz" and "Prologue as Part of the Body"; *The Southern Review*: "The Guineveres" (as "In the Blood") and "Modifying the Badger"; *Utne Reader*: "An Arrangement of Skin" (reprint).

Profound gratitude to my stellar agent Chris Clemans at the Clegg Agency for his invaluable insights, encouragement, and essential role in helping me shape this collection. Thanks to Rolph Blythe and to all of the folks at Counterpoint Press: Megan Fishmann, Nick Gomez-Hall, Joe Goodale, Bethany Onsgard, Shannon Price, and Kelly Winton. Thanks to Sven Birkerts, Jennifer Alise Drew, and

Bill Pierce at *AGNI* for their crucial support and editorial advice. Thanks to Mark Doty, Kwame Dawes, Jessica Faust, Mary Flinn, Nick Flynn, Maggie Nelson, and Emily Nemens. Thanks to Ryan McLennan for generously allowing me to reproduce his painting, *The Penitent and the Patient*, on the cover of this book.

"Prologue as Part of the Body" takes its title from the eponymous poem by Beckian Fritz Goldberg and is dedicated to the tattoo artist Captain Morgan.

Love and gratitude to David St. John, my extraordinary husband and first reader.

AN ARRANGEMENT OF SKIN

AN ARRANGEMENT OF SKIN

The man on the other end of Houston's local suicide hotline said his name was Blain. He had the nasal voice of a Texas weatherman: its kazoo-like lilt and swampy, Gulf Coast slowness. "I guess you know why I'm calling," I said. Blain said he did not know and why didn't I tell him. I told Blain that my life was falling apart. I told Blain how clichéd it was that I just said that, and I was a poet and hated clichés. I told Blain that every citizen in my former city—Richmond, Virginia—and my current one—Houston, Texas—was now aware of the affair I'd had before the breakup of my seven-year relationship. That the day after the blowout in which my newly minted ex, Carrick, kicked me out of our apartment, I'd defended my dissertation in a circle of English professors at the University of Houston in a pursed-smile stupor. "What does the color red symbolize in your work, Anna?" Dr. Serrano had asked me, cocking her head. I wanted to rip the blinds from the office window. I wanted to shout, "This is how I feel about red!"

Afterward, instead of celebrating my years of hard work in graduate school and the fact that I could now plunk "Dr." in front of my own name, I returned to collapse on a friend's mattress, with her silver tabby, Slider, watching the cat chase phantom mice among the amber patches of her quilt.

I told Blain how one of my closest friends, Lee, had ratted me out to Carrick and gossiped to our acquaintances. Lee had been my literary mentor and surrogate uncle throughout college, the person who'd first introduced me to poetry—my passion and my vocation. We'd spent hours talking about poetry: sitting in his office where even the faux fireplace gaped with books; hiking along trails and icy Appalachian creeks in Sugar Hollow; sipping coffee at orange tables with mismatched fifties chairs in the punk-rock diner on Cary Street, the walls patchworked with graffiti-inspired paintings and studded with antique dolls' heads. I loved Lee's wild stories: how the FBI tapped his phone in the seventies after he'd organized campus protests against the Vietnam War; how he once went whitewater rafting with a Utah cowgirl; how he rented an apartment in London for two weeks only to discover he'd be rooming with the English actor Ben Cross. Not only were my relationship and my long-valued friendship broken, I felt as if poetry itself was broken—that my writing and the person who had first nurtured it had deserted me. The magic that used to infuse the fables and myths in my poems now seemed as extinct as the dodo or as impossible as the unicorn.

I told Blain that in the dregs of my guilt, before I'd been outed for the affair, I'd invented a ritual to stop time. When Carrick zipped his upright bass into its black canvas case the size of a body and drove off in his station wagon for a weekend gig with a string band in Austin, I was relieved to have the apartment to myself for a few days so I didn't have to fake feeling normal. I didn't have to send text messages with the door locked and the shower running. I didn't have to sit on the porch, looking up at the lawn's gnarled live oak where even the silver Spanish moss seemed truly metallic, too heavy for the tree's arms to hold. Late one night I left the quiet of the apartment and bought a five-dollar egg timer from the twenty-four-hour Kroger on West Gray. As I paid for the timer I managed to make cheerful small talk with the ponytailed cashier amid the unforgiving chisel of the grocery store's halogen lights. I walked back through the dark Texas streets tiered in ratty date palms, battered tea roses, and scumbled rows of oleanders barely lit in their own fuchsia glow. At home I opened the plastic clamshell packaging and sat the egg timer on top of a swan's nest of yellow bath towels lumped on the floor. I cranked the Rolling Stones from my cheap speakers. I synced the coarse voice of Keith Richards and the driving snare drum toward the end of "Thru and Thru" with my timer's shrill alarm, which I'd coordinated to coincide with the precise tick of midnight. I smashed the ringing clock with a claw hammer until I broke through the white plastic, until there was nothing left to break there at the empty center of the sound.

. . . .

"The secret wish of all poetry is to stop time," says poet Charles Simic. I've wanted to still a moment before, the way the sycamore-spotted birthmark on my inner thigh looks like a continent about to divide itself; the time my mother discovered my grandfather's gay porn stash while cleaning out his house in Jackson after his death; the way a crawdad will hold its pinch until it hears thunder, according to those shivery Southern myths whispered in the dark of the porch. I've felt stilled by poems before, writing them and reading them. Haven't we all felt like this, though, even when we're feeling entirely unpoetic? Even when we're vindictive and terrified and enraged and small? Hasn't the world slowed to an acute and clarifying bluntness as we dropped an exposed toothbrush on an airport bathroom's queasy-green tile, or as we skidded into a pick-up's bumper, or as we hung up the phone, that voice saying good-bye in anger reverberating like the end of Pangaea, that ancient landmass ripping and rifting forever?

"The lyric moment is an eternal moment," poet Kathleen Graber suggests, "one that resurrects and resanctifies what has been lost. To stop time and to experience one moment of stillness. What is more impossible, more desired, than that?"

. . . .

I don't know why on my first trip to Paris last summer, at thirty-one years old, I chose to visit a dusty 180-year-old house of taxidermy over the grandeur of the Louvre or Versailles. Several months after my conversation with Blain, I'd fled the smother-ing white oak swamps of East Texas for the sunny perkiness of Southern California. I began teaching and slowly winding my way back to poetry. I watched my students' eyes flash with surprise as we discussed a poem by Jack Gilbert in which a lonely man sits in his kitchen projecting a pornographic film onto the surface of a plum, as if in doing so he might contain a diffuse, unruly desire. I watched my office door creak open as a student entered, eager and shy and falling in love with writing the way I had a decade earlier.

Not long after I moved to Venice Beach, with its Craftsman-style bungalows and dazzling rows of duck-cruised canals, I mar-ried a deeply kind man—and fellow writer—near the edge of a seaside cliff on Catalina Island, where the leggy newlywed teen Norma Jeane Baker (the future Marilyn Monroe) once lived for a year and where the actress Natalie Wood slipped from her yacht to drown in her down jacket and dark curls. I felt drawn to Catalina for its glamorous past; its tragic women; its uneasy, isolated beauty. And though I'd grown happier and more stable since contemplating suicide, I'd never quite rid myself of the hauntedness—that spidery guilt, humiliation, and defeat webbing me even amid the salt-and-jasmine sea breezes and easy West Coast light.

. . . .

Deyrolle is part Parisian taxidermy shop, part museum of oddities situated on a bustling strip of the Left Bank's rue du Bac—a street swarming with slim, speed-walking women in ballet flats and stubbled men in cashmere scarves. Deyrolle is a portal into another, stiller world: that calm and timeless center within a glitzy, temporal swirl. The shop's double doors and front windows gleam in oiled mahogany, trimmed with gold paint, and inside someone's sponged all the walls a mild lima-bean green. The second story houses Deyrolle's collection of taxidermied animals and insects. A few hunting trophy heads of deer and buffalo stud the walls, but the four rooms are mostly filled with creatures frozen in realistic poses: a white peacock and its blue-and-green counterpart sit side by side on perches in a corner, facing the wall in order to better spread their tail feathers for visitors; a honey badger with a dropped jaw raises one front paw as if to step miraculously from its display log; a spiny anteater hangs from a branch with its taupe muzzle poking out at passersby. In one side room, narrow as an old railway car, an array of vintage pedagogical boards adorn the walls and peep from cabinets: framed diagrams of grey-fluted mushrooms; pictures of the labor of honeybees in their golden hives; prints of the delicate skeletal structures of frogs that look as if someone lifted the lid to an amphibious piano to reveal its secret machinery. In a large middle chamber are displays of shells, corals, and crustaceans, interrupted here and there by the jut of a stuffed zebra, an upright polar bear, or a pair of chestnut-colored capybara that resemble ancient, knee-high horses with rounded snouts. Several of the rooms also contain boxes of minerals (quartz, gypsum, European granite); and the final back gallery offers the shop's entomological collection: white butterflies with wings the sheen of mother-of-pearl; a cicada mounted next to its own crepe-thin shell on a piece of shellacked bark; fat scorpions with black tails poised to strike. Deyrolle is almost entirely walled with glass-fronted wooden cabinets of curiosities. The shelves are stacked with sepia-flecked ostrich eggs mounted on pewter stands, collages made of layered monarch wings that radiate an odd poignancy, anatomical charts on the red and threadlike neural systems of spiders, corked apothecary vials of sea horses that have the matte patina of dried honeycombs. The curio cabinets make up Deyrolle's *Wunderkammer*, or "wonder-rooms."

. . . .

I've learned that the word "taxidermy" comes from the Greek *taxis* ("arrangement") and *derma* ("skin"), and may be defined, literally, as "an arrangement of skin." In addition to being well-versed in the details of anatomy and the craft of tanning, taxidermists must also work to evoke that ineffable spark of life: call it a soul, a personality, a sentience. If we see a bit of batting poking from a belly seam or an amber dab of dried glue oozing from the side of a glass eye, the spell is broken and the work recedes into lifelessness. And taxidermy is about life, not death. I've realized this slowly, staring at the miniscule bristles and graceful angles of limbs. It's about the ability to look closely and patiently at the body of an animal. The taxidermist represents not the dead creature, but the living one, held in time, for just an instant. Taxidermy creates the illusion that an animal's movement has only momentarily been stilled.

. . . .

Ten years ago, when I took my first undergraduate poetry class at Virginia Commonwealth University, in Richmond, I slept with a plastic bottle of Ambien on my bedside table to remedy my insomnia. At least that was what I told my friends, and even myself. Occasionally, I could feel that awful secret as it twinged hotly on my tongue, like a clove-spiced lozenge. I realized that keeping the sleeping pills within my reach was my own perverse sort of insurance policy: my escape in case I finally decided to swallow a handful. Whenever the pull grew too strong, I'd flush them.

The pull grew less strong as I discovered poetry: how Sylvia Plath's speaker brags in "Lady Lazarus" about her phoenix-like capacity for resurrection and triumph from suicidal catastrophe: "Out of the ash / I rise with my red hair / And I eat men like air." Or how Charles Wright imagines a constellation shaped like a swirling, ethereal spider—"juiced crystal and Milky Way"—and traces how we seek transformative beauty in the details of our daily lives: "All morning we look for the white face to rise from the lake / like a tiny star. / And when it does, we lie back in our watery hair and rock."

. . . .

The stone crab at Deyrolle seems to float in a coral cloud of its own body parts behind a cube of Plexiglas. It's the size of a dinner plate and dangles in evenly spaced segments, like a marionette, joined by pencil-thick lengths of copper wire. Its jagged orange pinchers, fractured and reassembled, point to the sky. The stone crab holds a shape impossible in life. It's as if it had dropped from a great height, and, just at the moment of impact, just as the fragments of shell began to roll away from each other, someone froze time. Below the crab crouches a cat-sized taxidermied skunk with hair wispier and more delicate than I'd imagined such a feral critter having. Its black-and-white stripes mingle into a narrow patch of silver in the once-wind-tussled arch of its spine, as if a strange breeze had just blown up the spiral staircase of the shop and passed by.

. . . .

In his famous essay, "Some Reflections on Dolls," early-twentieth-century Bohemian-Austrian poet Rainer Maria Rilke voices his antipathy toward dolls. According to Rilke, those lifelike objects trick us, as children, into inventing souls for them, a process that later results in feelings of disillusionment and betrayal. Once the child realizes that her toy has outgrown her sympathies, the fig-ure's dark, disenchanting nature "would break out," Rilke writes, "it would lie before us unmasked as the horrible foreign body on which we had wasted our purest ardor; as the externally painted watery corpse, which floated and swam on the flood-tides of our affection, until we were on dry land again and left it lying forgot-ten in some undergrowth." To Rilke, the relationship connecting a child and a doll unravels, over time, into a sinister one.

. . . .

Yet that's not why I could no longer look with easy affection at my own favorite stuffed animal from childhood, Charlie: that golden lab puppy my mother bought me instead of a live dog when I was in third grade. During the same humid Houston fall that I'd phoned Blain, I'd also confessed regularly into the ear of the stuffed dog. It sounds suspect, but I wasn't hallucinating. I didn't believe the dog would talk back. I must've needed a way to enact a dialogue with my own mind: Should I kill myself? What about my parents, my little sister, my best friend in Oregon with her new baby? How could Lee so self-righteously rat me out, sever our friendship and the link that connected me to my first experience of poetry? And how could I be a good writer and teacher of poetry if I constantly heard the harsh, judgmental rasps of my old mentor thrumming in my skull? Was I unforgivable?

I whispered to Charlie about how I'd told Blain my fantasy of checking into the campus Hilton, locking myself in the bathroom, and swallowing a handful of Ambien. When Blain asked me to consider the shock of the housekeeper who'd discover my body, how the trauma would affect that person, I paused to picture the scene. First, I might as well order room service and have the butter-poached lobster and a pomegranate martini—a sort of "last call" for pleasure, courtesy of the material world. I'd then write a note and tape it to the bathroom door, warning the cleaning crew of the room's grisly contents, thereby warding off the horror of an unanticipated discovery. I'd write the note in both English and Spanish, just to be sure. I'd print the words because my cursive is clumsily elephantine from my only using it to sign cover letters for poetry submissions or checks to renew my *New Yorker* subscription each October. I wouldn't use any hotel towels. I'd keep the hem of the shower curtain free of the bathtub. I'd leave a big cash tip by the phone. I pictured myself curling up in the tub, with an inch or two of warm water drawn for comfort. I could just let myself wander off. As my breathing slowed I'd slump lower in the tub, my red hair spoking from my pale face like mad Ophelia's waves in the Danish brook. The way the flat practicalities of my plan pitched into an idealized—even precious—morbidity jarred and disgusted me. I wouldn't be at all like Shakespeare's Ophelia, floating eternally and lovely and tragic: I'd just be dead. I promised Blain I wouldn't be booking an eternal stay at the campus Hilton anytime soon.

. . . .

I stood a long time in front of the pair of taxidermied peacocks at Deyrolle. I liked the way someone had positioned the white peacock next to the bird with saturated hues, as if the anemic one were dreaming sideways and in a cascade of color. Or vice versa: the blue-and-green peacock looked back on the distant winter of his own mind to find that—yes—he'd survived. The pairing reminded me I now stood on the other side of that November in Houston, safe on a whole other coast and in a new quality of light.

. . . .

Since 1831, the principle of Deyrolle has been "to bring to human nature the sense of observation and description"; that "if one wants to protect nature, one has to know it." Instead of an Eiffel Tower postcard, I chose a baby scorpion as a souvenir of my first trip to Paris. I thought the larger arachnids, with their curled fat tails, might break during my flight back to California. The bespectacled man behind the counter in the entomology room, who'd gently scolded me a few minutes earlier for photographing the stone crab, pinned my scorpion inside a small cardboard box and padded its body in cotton. His pupils looked unusually dilated, as if his daily peering into the minute details of shining beetles and rare butterflies had forever magnified his gaze. I wondered, as I descended the stairs to the street, if the airport security guards at US Customs would linger over the X-ray of my bags; if they'd ever seen a woman carrying a baby scorpion in her purse; if, as their scanners turned objects transparent, they'd glance at me; if they'd ask me how many times in this life I'd been stung, and with what difficulty, perhaps, I had managed to survive.

. . . .

In "Some Reflections on Dolls," Rilke addresses the deceitful doll-soul, as if he held the shell of it—that silent object—in his hands:

> O soul, that has never been really worn, that has only been kept always stored up (like furs in summer), protected by all kinds of old-fashioned odors: look, now the moths have got into you. You have been left untouched too long, now a hand both careful and mischievous is shaking you—look, look, all the little woebegone moths are fluttering out of you, indescribably mortal, beginning, even at the moment when they find themselves, to bid themselves farewell.

As I wandered the wonder-rooms of Deyrolle, I imagined the inverse of Rilke's disillusionment in which moths flutter terribly mortal—from the body of the shaken doll. I imagined each creature held a history inside it, the intricacies of a lived life, with its shifting landscapes and loves. I imagined the spiny anteater licking garnet clusters of ants, flicking its lavender tongue, and the yellowed ivory of a nineteenth-century fox skeleton in a bell jar beginning to shiver and plink out its story of longing for a red barn and a farmer's chicken coop. I imagined the white peacock perfectly camouflaged on a blizzard-encrusted stump, as if the snow had grown a miraculous bird of powder-white plumes, who now rises—resurrected—from the shining, winter ice.

There, almost two years on the living side of that divide I had faced in Houston, I could also imagine how my act of looking—the care with which I engaged the world, that alertness and openness and sensitivity—was a way to beat back the seductiveness of death. When I stepped into Deyrolle, the magic and energy of lives pulsed around me: countless species and shells and wings and the most complexly beautiful—and fragile—skeletons. I felt wonderstruck. These specimens of stopped time were, I realized, transparent, undying. Deyrolle was like an ark that carried me—carries all of us, our stories. I felt that world I had once tried to pry apart within the egg timer finally open up and let me—still breathing—step inside.

BIRDS 101

The skin of a dead starling is hardier than you'd think. It's tissue-fine yet lizard-like—wheat-colored chain mail for an airborne knight. During my first class at Prey Taxidermy, in downtown Los Angeles, I could see in the slit breast of my specimen a mix of delicacy and toughness, the bird's firm insides cool from the freezer and as flush as a plum.

Allis Markham, the owner of Prey, is a wisecracking thirty-two-year-old with fair skin and dyed-black hair. Around the studio, she wears a ponytail and simple button-up with rolled sleeves, but in a glamorous portrait on Prey's website, Allis poses between two taxidermied housecats like a deadpan 1940s pinup star: carmine lipstick and a dark rockabilly pompadour. In 2008, Allis (pronounced "Alice") quit her marketing job at Disney, where she earned a six-figure salary, to attend the Advanced Taxidermy Training Center in Montana. In her studio on the fourth floor of an arts building on Spring Street, Allis offers a range of weekend workshops for an array of misfits, hipster craftspeople, Hollywood types—and the plain old morbidly curious, like me. I decided to take Allis's recommended course for beginners, Birds 101.

. . . .

As a child, I kept a number of pets: a strawberry-blond hamster, a pair of parakeets, a fire-bellied newt, a short-lived guppy, several generations of sweet-tempered mice, a frisky rat, and three beloved indoor cats. A collector of rocks and fossils, I'd ride the metro into DC to visit the Smithsonian Museum of Natural History as often as my parents would take me. If I could've purchased taxidermy from the museum's gift shop in addition to geodes, arrowheads, and dime-sized trilobites, I would've transformed my bedroom into a wondrous forest populated with a hawk on my bookcase, a lemur on my lamp, a lynx in a corner, and a fox on the edge of my bedframe, one paw lifted midair, like a tightrope walker. Instead, I settled for a lucky rabbit's-foot keychain from the pet store at Twinbrook Shopping Center. Marveling at the paw's dry ivory fur, four lead-colored nails, and stiff dewclaw split to the quick, I considered the foot too precious to dangle from my backpack's zipper. I chose to display it on my bookshelf near my collection of miniature china animals with lapis paisleys painted in intricate wisps across their backs. My dad bought me a new blue-and-white figurine from the airport each time he flew on business trips to Thailand, Singapore, or Nairobi. My favorite one was a hippo with the tip of its pale snout dipped in a rich navy glaze. I handled the animal so often that I chipped off both of its ears. I clipped photographs of birds, mammals, and reptiles from my father's stacks of *National Geographic* magazines, taping the creatures over every inch of my walls—and the swaths of ceiling I could reach—to weave a patchwork menagerie.

Visiting the famous Parisian shop of curiosities, Deyrolle, on a trip to Europe with my husband several summers ago, I reawakened my interest in taxidermy. And as I neared the end of my first year of teaching full time, sitting quietly through departmental meetings and writing scrupulous comments on my students' essays and poems, I longed to rebel—to do something rougher, more insubordinate or wild. I became fascinated by taxidermy's paradoxical intents: to use dead matter to defy the natural outcome of mortality (vanishing) and to celebrate through the gestures of a corpse the wonders, textures, and varieties of life.

Finally, my husband searched on the Internet for local taxidermists, found Allis's studio, and turned the screen of his laptop toward me. I'd assumed most practitioners of taxidermy were gun-loving middle-aged men dressed in camouflage looking to make shoulder mounts of their shot whitetails. I knew, as I peered at Allis's website, that my perceptions had been skewed. Almost all of the students in her photographs—grinning next to their skunks, coyotes, and raccoons—were young women.

. . . .

In *The Breathless Zoo: Taxidermy and the Cultures of Longing*, writer and curator Rachel Poliquin argues that any of seven "narratives of longing" can move a person to create taxidermy: "wonder, beauty, spectacle, order, narrative, allegory, and remembrance." It's the manner in which we make meaning from these objects—the tales they allow us to tell about ourselves—that turns the taxidermist into a storyteller. That formerly blood-filled, hungry beast, now arrested in time and posed to emulate everlasting life, grows into a locus of ambiguity—it's both *here* and *not here*. Body without sentience. Is this once-breathing entity still an animal? Glass-eyed and lung-less, is it now an object? Can it straddle both categories, slipping back and forth, or has it broken down, irrevocably, and become neither? "What's my narrative of longing?" I wondered several weeks after I'd stuffed my starling, mounted the bird on a gnarled ghostwood branch, created a habitat using blue stones and pieces of driftwood, and placed all of it beneath a glass doll dome—the bird's low sky transparent and impervious, an eternal weather.

. . . .

On Saturday morning, students started to trail into Prey Taxidermy in the twenty minutes before class began. A brass moose head with a rusted patina and wide hoop dangling from its septum served as a door knocker. The suite of three rooms recalled the shape of an "L": the main workspace formed the base of the letter and two small rooms off the hallway made up the stem. The studio's white walls, tall windows, and minimal shelves recalled the curated space of an art gallery, though instead of paintings or sculptures, these rooms held sleek mounts of African ungulates (a gazelle, a dik-dik, and some type of massive antelope), a male peacock, the bust of a panda, several raccoons, and numerous birds.

Allis asked the ten students in Birds 101 to sit at either of two rectangular wooden tables in the workspace. In addition to Allis and her three apprentices (Ally, a sixteen-year-old who kept a pet Jacobin pigeon; Becca, a sixteen-year-old with fuchsia hair; and Jenn, a former paleontological field technician in her early thirties), there were nine women in their twenties and thirties and one teenage boy. Allis asked us to introduce ourselves and explain why we were taking the course. Arabella, a TV writer for a Golden Globe–winning series, wanted "to do something that doesn't involve words" and "to use [her] hands." Anne said she loved animals and worked in educational outreach at the Los Angeles Zoo. Olivia hoped to integrate taxidermy into her projects as a costume designer. The woman sitting next to Arabella, whose name I didn't catch, made jewelry from animal bones. At my table, Mitzy had pale blue hair with lavender streaks, and I can't remember if she gave a reason for taking the class. I introduced myself as a writer and mentioned my trip to Deyrolle. Ashley and Andrea were preppy architects who'd signed up for the class together. Andrea spoke about her interest in "freezing time." Sam, who sat across from me, had taken a previous course with Allis in which she'd taxidermied a spring duckling. She showed me a cell phone picture of her fluffy, butter-yellow bird, which appeared to waddle from its hillock of lime-green Astroturf as if into a book by Mother Goose. Sam said she liked the idea of "creating emotions beyond its life." Church, the only male in the class, was a scrawny junior in high school who wore chunky black-rimmed glasses. Without making eye contact with anyone, he hunched over the table and muttered something about taxidermy that I couldn't make out. Church's mother, Allis recalled, had taken Birds 101 before him.

Allis introduced us to our subject, the European starling: a stocky, eight-inch bird with a short tail, long yellow beak, and iridescent black feathers with glints of amethyst and sea green. Or as Steve Mirsky observes of the bird's dark and mottled patina in *Scientific American*: "they look like chocolate that's been left out for a few days." Although starlings may seem small in stature, they're gregarious, noisy birds, possessing strong feet for confident landings and an aggressive sense of curiosity. They're also gifted mimics, with a crackling, versatile song that swerves from a static-like rattle to a muddy gurgle to a piercing whistle-screech. They can imitate car alarms, jackhammers, even patterns of human speech. Deemed a nuisance species in the US, European starlings destroy nests ("Bad for local birds," said Allis) and ravage vineyards ("Which are *very* important to me," she added). Our specimens were "ethically sourced," she told us, which, in the parlance of taxidermy, means the birds weren't netted and gassed just to become rustic décor on our shelves. According to Allis, "Randy in Wisconsin" exterminated our starlings under the auspices of Pest Control.

We have a work of Elizabethan literature to blame for the starling's migration to the US during the nineteenth century: Shakespeare's history play, *Henry IV, Part 1*. According to Mirsky's article, a group of Shakespeare enthusiasts known as the Acclimatization Society vowed to populate North America with every species of bird the Bard cared to mention in his oeuvre—more than six hundred avian species. The nobleman Hotspur bitterly imagines driving the king crazy by training a starling to repeat the name of Mortimer, whom the king refuses to ransom. "I'll have a starling shall be taught to speak / Nothing but 'Mortimer,'" Hotspur says, and in response to these lines, the Acclimatization Society loosed a hundred starlings in Central Park in 1890 and 1891, tipping, in the name of literature, the balance of our ecosystem toward a raucous flock of proliferating black wings.

After Allis finished describing the difference between winter and summer plumage (white spots denote cold-weather feathers) and how beak length corresponds to age and hunting ability (bigger beaks mean older, seasoned feeders), we got to choose our starling from a group of eighteen corpses arranged on a counter in the hall. I approached the spread of specimens, which had been kept frozen, wings folded. They made me think of the ingredients to the teeming dessert described in "Sing a Song of Sixpence": "Four-and-twenty blackbirds / Baked in a pie." In the English nursery rhyme, when someone slices open the pie set before the king, a wily blackbird escapes from the crust, flies out the castle window, and pecks off the nose of a maid who'd been hanging laundry in the courtyard. I raised an eyebrow at the feathered pile and reached for a bird with dark summer plumage and a long vivid beak. An older one. A good feeder.

. . . .

There are eight distinct genres of taxidermy, suggests Rachel Poliquin: "hunting trophies, natural history specimens, wonders of nature (albino, two-headed, etc.), extinct species, preserved pets, fraudulent creatures, anthropomorphic taxidermy (toads on swings), and animal parts used in fashion and household décor."

My father, who grew up in Greenwood, Mississippi, once took a hunting trophy. In the rural South of the late 1950s, most men learned to hunt, and, even though my animal-loving father never much enjoyed it, he would grab his rifle and go on shooting trips with his friend Pete as a kind of bonding ritual. His friendship with Pete—and with Pete's gracious, educated parents—allowed my father passage, however temporarily, into a family far different from his own: one without his aloof, mean-tongued father, who ran a struggling well-digging business; without his older sister, Beulah, who was a violent bully; without his embittered mother, who, according to the town gossips, married late and "beneath her."

My father, prompted by my foray into taxidermy, wrote to tell me a story from his adolescence that I'd never heard before. When he and Pete were both fifteen, they came across an unusual fox squirrel in the kudzu-shrouded woods. Instead of red, the animal's fur was a rich, shiny black, and a stippling of white hairs surrounded its nose in a smoky halo. My father shot the squirrel and, because of its rare color, decided to preserve the pelt. He taught himself the process of tanning a hide by referencing his *Encyclopedia Americana*—what he called his "favorite resource for getting along with the world." Since fourth grade, he'd escaped Greenwood's dirt roads, rednecks, and desolate trailers through entering the alternate worlds created by reading and through hanging out with Pete's family. According to my father, he regularly shut himself in his room and read every volume in his encyclopedia set from cover to cover, like a novel, resulting in his impressive and enduring ability to recite curious facts, especially those concerned with science, history, and linguistics. (Over the course of a single weekend, for instance, he told me that "tattoo" is a Polynesian word; that kangaroos, unlike humans, are predominantly lefties; and that the decadent Chinese dish called "live monkey brain" requires a special table with a head-shaped hole cut in the middle so the doomed creature can sit beneath it, exposing its sawed-off cranium to diners wealthy enough to afford the appetizer.) To tan the hide, he measured out coarse salt and potassium nitrate and applied it to the cleaned squirrel, scraping off the mixture and reapplying it every few days until the skin was ready for moisturizing with mineral oil. "Tanning hides isn't taxidermy," my dad said, "but it's close."

. . . .

Bird skin doesn't require the tanning process, which is why it's perfect for beginning taxidermists, who can learn the basics of the craft in a single weekend. There are five steps involved in avian taxidermy: skinning, fleshing, wiring, mounting, and grooming. To prepare our starlings for skinning, we rinsed their bodies in the sink, to soften them and prevent brittleness and tearing. Back at our seats, the tables were set with metal lunch trays upon which rested a small handful of tools: a scalpel for slicing skin and sawing flesh from bone, a tweezer for prying off chunks of meat and tendons, a paintbrush for moisturizing dry patches, a wire brush for scouring yellow fat deposits, several small metal picks, and a large hooked dental tool known around the taxidermy studio as "the brain scoop." In the center of each table sat a rotating Lazy

Susan–style toolbox stocked with replacement blades, extra tools, and spools of wire and cotton thread. I sat my damp bird in the center of my tray, watched Allis demonstrate a blade change, and reached for my scalpel. I unpeeled the protective sheath of my blade halfway, held the sharp end by its wrapped tip, aligned the exposed dull end with a matching groove on the scalpel handle, and slid the blade down until I heard a firm click.

Following Allis's instructions, I spread the wings of my starling and used my pointer finger to feel for the divot in the bird's collarbone—the point at which the incision would begin. The first cut was surprisingly easy to make. The lightest pressure slit the skin of the starling's breast, without puncturing the muscle beneath. I ran my scalpel from the bird's collarbone down to its cloaca, the posterior opening for the intestinal, reproductive, and urinary tracts. Pulling back the starling's skin felt similar to pushing apart the fuzzy velveteen of a ripe peach. I thought the bird's guts would tumble out, but its muscles and organs stayed put, chilly and compact as a fist. There was very little blood—just the pink jellied fingerprints I kept smearing across the pages of my spiral notebook that browned in the air like the curled edges of roses. To skin the starling, I grasped the slimy edge of the incision between my left pointer finger and thumb, tugged upward, and used small strokes of the blade of my scalpel to sever the pearlescent networks of white microfibers—"the cobwebs"—that connected the skin to muscle. As more and more of my bird peeled open, I ran a water-dunked paintbrush over the underside of the skin dotted with yellow fat deposits. The chunks resembled remnants of caramel flan stuck to an aluminum baking pan. I also noticed bumpy follicles in which the tips of the feathers were rooted on the opposite side of the skin. "This is so meditative," one of the architects said, nose bent over her bird. Allis strolled around the room, peeking over our shoulders, and then switched the low-key indie rock playing on her Internet radio station to Ella Fitzgerald.

After skinning the bird's breast, I used my thumbs to pry out its plum-like interior: a process called "removing the body." "You'll hear a sound like Velcro," Allis said, "when you crack the patella." The bird's "knees," the assistant Jenn added, are in different places than our own—they're way up inside, like secret hips. "So don't think of your own anatomy while you do it," she urged. I found the hidden joints, cracked the patella with a satisfying crunch, changed my dull scalpel blade, and severed the pink, meaty region known as the "tail butt" from the lower vertebrae. I then tugged out the body—a pink and purple heart-shaped water balloon with a long pencil-neck—and snipped the top of the spine at the base of the skull with a wire cutter. I dropped the body into a white paint bucket for waste materials labeled "Meat Bucket."

After flipping the bird's neck inside out, like a wet sock, and scooting the skull down through the tube and out of the chest cavity, I had trouble locating the eyes and "releasing the ears." Birds do have ears, I discovered, though not external cartilaginous ones like ours. They have small oval holes on their heads hidden beneath their feathers. Jenn helped me skin around the ear holes and locate "the blueberries"—the eyes—one of which I accidentally popped in its socket with the tip of my scalpel. Gripping the firm stalks of the optic nerves with my tweezer, like the taproots of dandelions, I yanked them out and dropped my starling's pair of eyes—one whole and one punctured blueberry—into the meat bucket. I then scrubbed my hands and took my lunch break, unwrapping my turkey and Havarti on wheat.

. . . .

I stared at the raised paw of a taxidermied raccoon on the counter. As a kid, I got a thrill out of keeping a piece of something that had once been alive—that fact made its own kind of magic. But why exactly is a rabbit's foot lucky? "They're apotropaic," my father, still encyclopedic in his factoids, later informed me. The adjective describes something with the power to ward off evil or avert bad luck. "That's why we knock on wood," he said. That's why I picked four-leaf clovers from the special patch by my swing set or kissed my plaster life mask of John Keats before taking that English Romanticism exam, or why I bought on Etsy a skull-faced mermaid voodoo doll with a purple-sequined tail to which I could pin written wishes.

In *Lucifer Ascending: The Occult in Folklore and Popular Culture*, scholar Bill Ellis traces the mainstream popularity of lucky rabbits' feet during the twentieth century to fetish jewelers in the black districts of New Orleans. The superstition comes from African American *conjure* and concerns the belief that witches often shape-shifted into rabbits, so they could scamper around unnoticed, casting their evil spells. Ideally, Ellis notes, a hunter must use a silver bullet to shoot the supernatural creature. Cutting off a rabbit's foot (preferably in a cemetery, by the light of the moon), was a way to possess the magical bones of a witch, or contain one's own personal piece of wonderment, in order to manipulate and govern its intent.

· · · · · · · · · · ·

After lunch, we scooped the brains of our starlings to the jazz tunes of Ella Fitzgerald and Louis Armstrong. As the punchy, melodious duet "They Can't Take That Away from Me" began, I looked up to see if anyone else got the joke. Everyone was busy squinting and scooping in serious concentration. With the well-mannered jazz and craft tables and jabbing knives, our gathering could pass for a quilting bee directed by David Lynch.

My first sight of the starling's brain startled me: out came a tacky fuchsia ooze instead of the solid chunks of grey Jell-O I'd expected. "I thought it would look like a human brain," I said, "only smaller." Jenn said the brains liquefied after the birds were frozen. "I don't know why," she added. "Ice crystals," said the high schooler, Church, without looking up, as he stirred his bird skull with the scoop. "Ice crystals form and chop up the brain." This was the first thing Church had said in a while, aside from his shyly muttered introduction, and the women at our table glanced at him in surprise or amusement.

I continued to hear bits of conversation, likely unique to a taxidermy studio, that delighted me—especially the banter between Allis's neon-haired teenage apprentices, Ally and Becca: "I'm getting a piebald python." "One of the smoky ones?" "I like the high whites." "Is the accent on the second syllable of 'reticulated python' or the first?" "The most humane way to kill a rattlesnake is to freeze it." "Have you got rat feet down?" I also enjoyed the fact that Becca, skilled in the craft of skinning and stuffing beasts, slipped into the body of one each time she donned a cartoon rodent costume for her part-time job at Chuck E. Cheese's. "They won't let me wear my piercings inside the mouse suit," she sighed.

. . . .

The figure of the animal, from Chuck E. Cheese's furry burlesque to the apocalyptic fables of Ted Hughes's poetry collection *Crow*, continues to captivate our imaginations. The tradition of the beast fable is, in fact, one of our most ancient literary genres. In *A New Handbook of Literary Terms* scholar David Mikics defines the beast fable as "An economically told story with a moral, in which animals dramatize human faults." We can trace the genre's origins back to the ancient Greek writer Aesop, a storytelling slave who lived on the island of Samos during the sixth century BCE.

The most famous example of a beast fable in English may be Geoffrey Chaucer's *Nun's Priest's Tale*, composed in Middle English during the late fourteenth century. It tells the story of a sly, smooth-talking fox and an anxious, but ultimately clever, rooster. In the late seventeenth and eighteenth centuries, the genre surged in popularity due in part to the vast success of the French writer Jean de La Fontaine, who published the multiple volumes of his *Fables* from 1668 to 1694. Many of La Fontaine's fables, which he composed in verse, belong to the Aesopian tradition of anecdotal stories about animals endowed with human speech and who represent human qualities. In the opening poem of his epical twelve books, La Fontaine declares:

> I sing those heroes, Aesop's progeny,
> Whose tales, fictitious though indeed they be,
> Contain much truth. Herein, endowed with speech—
> Even the fish!—will all my creatures teach
> With human voice; for animals I choose
> To proffer lessons that we all might use.

. . . .

"Allis, will you look at my meat window?" I asked during the second day of class, employing the term for the vertical incision made along the middle joint of a bird's wing. I had picked the slit free of tendons and flesh, leaving, I supposed, the bones and surrounding skin as clean as the frame and panes of a freshly wiped window. After I'd "fleshed" my starling by hand as best I could, with my scalpel and wire brush, I took my specimen to one of the small rooms off the hallway, so I could use a machine called "the fleshing wheel" to grind off any remaining lumps of fat and to blast the tough-to-scrub area of the jagged tail butt. The fleshing wheel resembled a woodworker's lathe, with a hubcap-sized, rotating, circular wire brush under which I held my bird, watching, with satisfaction (and with my mouth shut), pink slivers of flesh go flying.

I packed my starling's empty skull and orbital sockets with clay, tamping it down with the brain scoop, and pushed the wired glass eyes into the clay, like ball-head pins. I then lathered my bird with green dish soap, rinsed it, rolled the damp body in a plastic bin of powdery "chinchilla fluff" (volcanic ash) to absorb any oil, and blow-dried the dusty feathers at an open window. As Church blasted his bird with a hair dryer beside me, he belted out show tunes from *Les Misérables*, his bird's wings and neck rippling and bobbing theatrically in his outstretched hand. Back at the table with our starlings, which were beginning to look like whole animals, we wired the legs and wings in order to pose them. Although I'd thought skinning and fleshing would be the most challenging parts of taxidermy, because of the guts and gore, it was the wiring process that had me grumbling "motherfucker" and cursing my bird. As I tried to feed the sharpened point of the wire through the hollow spaghetti-thin bones, I kept poking holes in the dry skeleton, bending the wire, and jabbing my own fingertips. Ally patiently tugged out my mangled wire, clipped new pieces, and helped me feed them through the joints of the wings until both limbs held their shapes. She also showed me how to wire the limp sock of the neck with a foam tube bent in the S shape of a plumbing pipe and stuff the chest with a cotton body. Because of my sewing experience, I neatly stitched up my starling's stuffed breast with a needle and black cotton thread.

. . . .

The final verse of "Sing a Song of Sixpence," in which the wounded maid whose nose was ripped off by the blackbird gets stitched back together, reminds me of sewing up the body of my starling: "They sent for the king's doctor, / who sewed it on again; / He sewed it on so neatly, / the seam was never seen." The taxidermist's ability to hide the seams—those threads that join dead flesh to fabric—is what makes the vanished animal flutter back to life. That surprise resurrection is precisely what underlies the whimsical recipe for a novelty dessert containing live birds described in the sixteenth-century Italian cookbook *Epulario*. When the pie was sliced and the songbirds burst out, the dinner guests would gasp and clap with delight. And although the origins of the nursery rhyme remain mysterious, according to the *Oxford Dictionary of Nursery Rhymes*, Shakespeare may be responsible for provoking the ditty. In *Twelfth Night*, Sir Toby Belch demands of a clown: "Come on; there is sixpence for you: let's have a song."

. . . .

After I'd taken home my bird, which I'd groomed to hide the pale slivers of down beneath black feathers (as the creature would do for itself in life) and wired its feet to a ghostwood branch, I tried to think of a name for it. My first instinct was to go for humor. The rhyming "Oh My Darling Starling," said quickly, with an Elvis drawl ("Oma Darlin' Starlin'"), came to mind. There was also the version that made use of my new jargon and carried an absurdist Cartoon Network–character flair: "Meat Window." I discovered, though, that neither name would stick. The bird appeared too dignified and realistically posed for my jokes. It seemed remote, bittersweet. It was always "the starling."

Poliquin observes the beast fable's humor is, necessarily, a dark one, rooted in the eat-or-be-eaten rule of survival—that brutal ethos of the barnyard. In taxidermy, she argues, humor often fizzles out because the moment of recognition so essential to fable—that instant we're able to see ourselves in the drama of the animals—is no longer accessible. We can no longer project ourselves into the world of the story because "[d]eath is too bluntly visible." Morals and movement recede into material fact (*this flesh is dead*), the smile fades, and the creature brings instead "a dark terminus to the fable tradition." As Poliquin reminds us: "the animals have lost the fight."

. . . .

In one of my father's stories—which, to me, feels like a beast fable—he and his friend Pete faced their blustery high school football coach, Jim Baddley, after practice. Coach Baddley hollered at the team, calling them "wormy slackers," and suggested that, since the boys were so dainty and delicate, he was beginning to believe they needed "fur-lined jock straps." My father glanced at Pete and folded his hands behind his back. When he got home, he rummaged in his desk for a box containing the rare black squirrel hide he'd tanned earlier that year. He claims he stayed up late, his door locked, gluing the hide to the cup of a jock strap and smoothing the folds to fit the concave angles. Several days later, my father presented the undergarment to Coach Baddley with a ceremonious bow, observing that, at his advanced age, it was *he* who would need a fur-lined jock strap to see him through the next football season. Fortunately for my dad, Coach Baddley howled uproariously, slapping him on the back, and showed off the contraption to the school's other coaches, vowing to wear it to the first game of the season.

"Most hunting stories have the same plot," Poliquin suggests. Certainly my father's heralded his pluck and pride. And although humor seemed to elide my attempts at naming my bird, my father was able to revise the ordinary narrative of his hunting trophy to create a wild fable infused with humor. In an era of 1950s conformity, he challenged an authority figure through his wit and resourcefulness. My father's story says, "I stood up for myself." The would-be Aesopian moral: "Brains over brawn." A fur-lined jock strap alters the fable of the squirrel pelt—that once-earnest object, that tangible proof of a vanquished foe—into a critique of conventional masculinity. The football field becomes a landscape of camp, a subversive burlesque. It's Mississippi surrealism in service of a young man's imaginative acts. And Coach Baddley recognized the value, as well as the humor, in that.

. . . .

My starling still doesn't have a name. I haven't given up, exactly; I've just grown okay with the ambiguity. It's "my bird" or "my starling." I believe the story it allows me to tell about myself may be a simple one: *Death scares me, but during those days at Prey I wasn't afraid to touch it.* For two nights in a row after the workshop I had skinning dreams, though I don't remember their plots—just flashes of skin and scalpels and those stretching cobwebs. I also began to look at my fat black cat differently. As I stroked Jellybean's belly, feeling her brisk heartbeat and ripples of skin, I thought, "You're a sack of guts covered in fur." Later, lying in bed reading, I absentmindedly felt my own right forearm. I turned to my husband. "My bones feel like *bones*," I said. I can now imagine what people's fat deposits look like on their inner thighs or buttocks, or how my own microfibers might shine in the bedside light. I think this is what doctors must conjure. Or morticians. Or cops. Hematologists must picture human-shaped knots of blood pushing carts at the grocery store. And in the bodies of shoppers who stoop to squeeze oranges in crates cardiologists must notice a floating row of beating hearts. I search for images or glints of story in a word or gesture: nine women and a boy deciding "winter or summer plumage" as they touch the bodies of their future birds; my father's hunting trophy turned fur-lined jock strap; Allis leaving the doe-eyed creatures of Disney for the grit and complexities of flesh. Those impossible resurrections—baked blackbirds flying from a pie. My bird is beautiful. I don't have a name for it. I opened it up and entered as if turning the first page of a story.

THE GOLIATH JAZZ

I.

I was a senior in high school, in May 1999, when my mother told me the curly-haired boy who'd once sung with me in our church's children's choir admitted to murdering his older sister in 1995 and burning down the family house. In a plea bargain with the DA, Matthew Harper had received thirty-five years without parole for bludgeoning his sister with a rolling pin; stabbing her in the back with a large kitchen knife and penetrating her heart; then setting the house on fire as their mother and grandmother slept. For a number of seconds I sipped my coffee without speaking. "Matt?" I finally asked. I hadn't thought about the Harper tragedy in years; and Matt's full name now sounded like a stranger's. "Matt who played David in *David and Goliath*?" The same fourteen-year-old boy I remembered singing the lead part in the Junior Choir's rendition of *David and Goliath* as the biblical hero who slays the ogreish Philistine warrior with a rock from his slingshot later murdered his sister, Anne Harper, on Thanksgiving morning, 1995. This was three years after his starring role in the musical sermon, at our Episcopalian church. After killing Anne—a twenty-year-old junior at Hollins College who'd returned to northern Virginia for the holiday—Matt poured gasoline around her body sprawled in the living room and went upstairs to dribble fuel oil outside of their mother's bedroom door. (Since the separation, their father had lived elsewhere.) Matt then set the redbrick house on Ryers Place ablaze. Although a neighbor was able to rescue the grandmother from her basement apartment, their mother Elizabeth Harper suffered first- and second-degree burns before she fell from a second-story window while trying to escape, breaking her back. She later refused to testify against her son. Matt was eighteen at the time he fled the burning house, flinging his blood-slick shoes into a shallow drainage creek.

． ． ． ． ． ． ． ． ． ． ．

As a shy, eleven-year-old fifth-grader, in the spring of 1992, I thought the eighth-grader Matt Harper the perfect sample of a teenage boy. I admired his dark, chin-length mane; his wry sense of humor; his confidence in leading the procession of red-and-white–robed choir members as we bobbed and trekked to our purple seats around the pipe organ; his starring role as the hero David, in his Birkenstocks and white socks. *David and Goliath* was my first church musical. Although no one in my immediate family is currently religious, my parents, who were both raised in Mississippi, dutifully brought my younger sister and me to the nine o'clock service at the Church of the Good Shepherd every Sunday morning. And though we lived in Fairfax, Virginia—a metropolitan suburb of Washington, DC—they felt that churchgoing was the proper Southern thing to do. When my mother gave me the choice between joining the Junior Choir Choristers or attending Sunday school, I picked singing over Bible study.

In *David and Goliath*, I played an Israelite whose homeland was threatened by the encroaching Philistine army. I sported braces with rubber bands the color of old chewing gum and bushy, hair-sprayed bangs that my father had trimmed, with the kitchen scissors, into the shape of a copper mushroom. For my costume I wore a magenta shirt with a purple-paisley "I," for "Israelite," appliquéd across my flat chest. I layered my magenta "I" T-shirt over a white turtleneck, while my friend Lisa—a Philistine—wore a lima-bean-green "P" T-shirt over her turtleneck. I blended in with the rest of the chorus, my soft, girl-soprano bleating a defiant taunt to Goliath as I shook my right fist: "We warn you, *Giiii*-ant! You're in a stew. You'll be a client for the undertaker's wagon when he's through with you."

In the musical, Goliath glided on wheels across the nave of the church, like a massive swivel chair—a hollow, ten-foot-tall puppet with facial hair and no visible hip bones or evident legs. Someone's dad had built the Philistine giant's plywood-framed body in the shape of a barrel with squared shoulders and a quarterback's fat neck. Someone else's parent had assembled Goliath's black-and-white muumuu using what looked like a bedsheet slung over an old Senior Choir robe. They'd draped his head in a grey cloth helmet and given his rectangular face two furrowed caterpillar eyebrows and a brown, pelt-like beard. For some reason Goliath didn't have any ears, eyeballs, or a nose. He resembled an obese, craft-fair soldier-nutcracker on roller skates or a Cold War–era cartoon of a dark-bearded Russki. Instead of stepping toward the shepherd David for a fight, Goliath—pushed from behind by a member of the cast—rattled on his wheels, like a refrigerator, toward Matt Harper, who I remember raised his slingshot. I don't remember whether Matt launched a foam rock. I do recall that instead of tumbling over when struck in the head, Goliath comically shrank to half his height, as if he'd been stomped on like an aluminum beer can. One tug of a wooden lever sent the top portion of the giant's torso sliding down over his bottom half, like the larger barrel of a telescope collapsing over the smaller. With Goliath dead, the Philistine army fled. The audience roared and clapped with delight.

. . . .

Anne Harper seems a more distant figure. Five years my senior, she sang in the ninth- through twelfth-grade choir called Lightshine and wore a navy robe cinched in the middle with tasseled gold ropes. I often watched her from my seat on the opposite side of the pipe organ. Anne had long, strawberry-blond hair and fair skin— like mine—and our first names differed by only a single letter. The image of Anne continues to linger in my memory, while the rest of the teenage singers in Lightshine have long vanished from their seats beneath the organ's symmetrical lead pipes. Sometimes I'd look up from my plum-colored hymnal and catch Anne's eye. She had a slender, pointed nose; wide hips; thick, slightly messy hair; and, without much makeup, a subtly old-fashioned paleness in her dark robe. Anne could've been cast as an extra in a movie about pioneers moving west in covered wagons. She'd smile at me through her bangs, though she didn't have braces. I wondered if she might be what I'd eventually look like as a teenager.

. . . .

In February 1992, a couple of months before Matt cracked Goliath in the head with a rock from his slingshot to cheers and applause, Anne reflected on the aftermath of her parents' separation in her diary. Journalist Tom Jackman quotes several of Anne's entries in the *Washington Post*. "Mom and Matt raised voices 'cause he wants to stay with Dad," she writes. "Matt punched a hole in the wall and cracked a door. Scary." In other entries presented in the trial, Anne writes chillingly of Matt's violence toward their mother: "Mom and Matt got into an awful fight today. . . . It got physical. Mom has an awful red mark on her R eye, and for a while her lower face (R) was swollen." Elsewhere in her diary Anne notes Matt's growing combativeness. "Matt and I had a major fight—one of the biggest in years," she confides. "He's been so damn aggressive toward me lately," she writes on another date. "Why? I haven't done anything."

. . . .

Because of my shyness, our choir director, Marti, declined to cast me as the notorious Phoenician queen, Jezebel, in a later church musical. Instead, she gave the role to Louise, who often showed up late to Wednesday-evening choir practice still wearing her junior high school cheerleading uniform. I received my usual role as a member of the chorus. "Now Jezebel was their queen," I sang, waving my jazz hands in Louise's direction. "A meaner queen you've never seen. She prayed daily to a stone god. She bowed and scraped and acted odd." The role of Jezebel was everything I wasn't: flamboyant, loud, sexy, defiant. I thought, though, if given a chance, I might morph into the role, embrace Jezebel's traits, and belt out her solo as she's dragged by members of her court toward an open window to be tossed to the wild dogs: "This time tomorrow, you'll be dead, so dead. Enough is enough! Hear what I've said: This time tomor-*ro-ho*, you'll be dead!"

. . . .

"When I think about my sister, I think of a beautiful young woman," Matthew Harper said in front of a packed courtroom, in May 1999, after receiving his prison sentence for second-degree murder and arson: thirty-five years without the possibility of parole. For the past few years, as detectives built a case against him, Matt had majored in psychology at James Madison University in Harrisonburg. He continued to attend classes at JMU, even after his first-degree murder indictment, and to visit his family, who'd posted his bond and refused to believe he'd murdered his sister. Matt finally confessed to killing Anne when he attended a court hearing at which prosecutors presented evidence that suddenly called up, he said, repressed memories of the crime. As part of the plea deal, the DA had reduced the first-degree murder charge to second degree and had dropped the attempted murder charge. "I miss her every day," Matt continued. "I can't believe I took her life, but I know that I did." It was his first public statement about his sister's death.

I recall thinking that a sentence of thirty-five years seemed like a long time for a crime of passion, which is what I supposed the killing to be. Why else would an eighteen-year-old boy whack his sister in the head with a rolling pin and stab her in the back with a kitchen knife? Hadn't my mother mentioned Matt's alleged cocaine use and history of sibling rivalry? Maybe Anne came down the stairs, at two in the morning, and surprised Matt in the kitchen. Maybe he was balancing a bump of coke on the tip of a credit card or going through her purse. He must've been out of his mind when the argument started. The rolling pin and knife sitting right there, on the counter, ready for the Thanksgiving piecrusts.

. . . .

Although my mother saved the program for *David and Goliath* and a number of photographs of the musical sermon, I've longed to find a videotape of the production. I remember a black tripod in the back of the nave, with the wide eye of a camera, recording away. I want to see for myself Matt singing the part of David, Matt killing Goliath, me looking with admiration on the star of the play, the savior of the Israelites and the whole day. I want to find out if I can "see" anything in him, any hint of what's to come. Wasn't anyone paying attention, besides Anne? And was she watching from the audience as Goliath imploded in what must've been a comic gesture to nearly everyone and a *danse macabre* to Anne and her mother? Wasn't anyone else, over twenty years ago, able to ask, as Anne had: "Why?"

II.

It's Thanksgiving morning, eighteen years to the day Anne Harper died, and I've received from my father, via e-mail, nine scanned photographs of the musical sermon as well as the program my mother located. I got it all wrong. Instead of *David and Goliath*, the musical has the campier, Broadway-esque title, *The Goliath Jazz*. As I glance at the program, I find Matt Harper's name, at the top, right beneath the name in all caps: "GOLIATH." Matt never played David. He was, after all, the villain. Why had I so confidently, and over so many years, remembered otherwise? Why had I cast Matt as the hero? There is his name, though, printed in the old program, and there is his titular role as Goliath—the single and central name. Why did I remember "his dark, chin-length mane" when, in the only clear photograph I have of Matt, his blunt hairstyle is so clearly a frizzy mullet? He also wears hubcap-shaped, amber glasses. I almost didn't notice Matt as I scrolled through the nine photographs, but there he is, in two of them. In one photograph—which shows the entire magenta-and-lima-bean-green cast holding hands and raising their arms for a group bow—the belled, red sleeve of the real David obscures Matt's face. (According to the program, a girl named Valerie had played David; she'd slicked her shoulder-grazing blond hair back in a French braid.) In the other photograph, Matt has just slipped from his place behind the ten-foot Goliath, after pulling the lever that caused the giant to collapse to half his former height. Matt wears a white T-shirt with a black "G," for Goliath, patched to the middle of his chest.

....

According to an article by Katherine Lenker, published in JMU's newspaper, *The Breeze*, Matt Harper initially claimed that he'd been in bed at his girlfriend's house at two A.M. when his mother discovered the fire in the early hours of Thanksgiving day. At four A.M., Matt and his girlfriend met his injured mother in her room at Fairfax Hospital. (His grandmother had escaped the blaze unharmed.) Several emergency room employees noticed traces of soot around Matt's nose and mouth, and they observed a strained dynamic between mother and son. "Their interaction seemed unnatural and lacking in emotions," one nurse said. Investigators also found soot stains smeared into the girlfriend's pillowcase. Matt claimed to have gotten soot on his face from embracing his mother while she lay in her hospital bed, but the nurses testified that he'd never once hugged her.

....

The musical score of *The Goliath Jazz* looks like a relic from the 1970s, which is precisely what it is. I bought a copy of it online. The slim, cream-colored booklet is covered in bubbly chocolate-brown and yellow biblical cartoons, including one of Goliath in his helmet and cumulous beard and a tiny, squirrel-sized David leaping above the giant's shoulder, swinging his slingshot. Inside the booklet, Tracey Lloyd's and Herbert Chappell's lyrics haven't aged especially well. Exclamatory onomatopoeia abounds: "Zam! Kersplatt! Ker-joing! And Pow!" And the jokes must've always been groaners:

GOL: I say, I say, I say.
I've got a goat with no nose.
DAV: You've got a goat with no nose?
GOL: I've got a goat with no nose.
DAV: Then how does it smell?
GOL: Terrible!

Other lines from *The Goliath Jazz*, in the context of Anne's murder, resonate with a grim irony or an eerie prescience. "I prefer to pick on someone more my height," sneers Goliath when confronted by the tiny Israelite. Later, Goliath warns: "From here on in it's murder, Mister."

. . . .

When detectives questioned Matt about the crime, he suggested the killer was the same person who'd broken into the garage and stolen his expensive road bike. The police later discovered that Matt had in fact sold the bike to a consignment shop, filed a burglary report, and received a $3,600 payment from an insurance claim. Deputy Commonwealth's Attorney Raymond Morrogh argued in court that Matt's motivation for the murder was financial, citing Matt's suspicious history of filing insurance claims, including one for a bike that had burned "accidentally" the summer before the murder. Matt received an insurance settlement for that bike as well. Detectives uncovered three other claims that the insurance company refused to pay because of Matt's failure to cooperate with the company's investigations. Maybe Anne heard a noise in the middle of the night and got up to find Matt dousing the house with accelerant, Morrogh theorized. According to the *Washington Post*, Matt had told a friend that, due to his family members' insurance policies, "if everyone in his family died, he'd get over $1 million."

. . . .

I have trouble reconciling what I remember about Matt with what must have been true: that he could shove the wheeled Goliath puppet through the church's nave as easily as he could punch a hole through the wall of his house. How could he play the roles of both choirboy and bully who bruised the right eye of his mother? Those roles would've been, according to Anne's diary, simultaneous. How could he change, in just three years, from campy biblical monster to real-life murderer? I should have scrutinized Anne more deeply as she sat across from me at the pipe organ. She was more than a mirror of my own narcissistic teenage potential. She was a young woman who loved cathedrals, who'd soon major in medieval studies and spend a semester in Europe, who'd continue singing as a member of the chapel choir at Hollins. All I have left of her is a few scattered diary excerpts, cited in old newspapers and floating among the debris of the Internet's now ancient corners. And why didn't I see Anne flinch as the bass notes of the organ mimicked the sudden echo of a male voice behind her, or notice the right side of her mother's face, dark behind its thick foundation?

I could hardly believe this sentence about Matt printed in JMU's *The Breeze*: "Harper was also involved in the Vestry, the leadership group of Canterbury Episcopal Campus Ministry." Until he was finally arrested during his eight A.M. Sign Language class, in 1998, three years after the murder, Matt continued to play a role in the Episcopal church. He represented himself as a Christian "leader" and model college student, even after he'd left his sister, mother, and grandmother to the flames and ashes of a burning house. No photographs of Matt Harper (or Anne Harper), as far as I know, are available on the Internet—just this one scanned image in my inbox that contains Matt's upper body and face. If I zoom in on his picture, I can correct his hairstyle in my memory. I can reassign him his right part. I understand that, from the very start, he'd always been Goliath. Why is it I still see him, though, so clearly and wrongly as the hero, leaning back to face the giant, calm and lethal, just beginning to take aim for his shot?

....

I can't erase the old Junior Choir songs from my memory. I can't get them out of my head. Most of the tunes are innocuous, melodic, reverent, nostalgic. Most of them are Christmas carols, hypnotic psalms, Easter hymns, slapstick musical numbers. But the ones from *The Goliath Jazz* burn on my tongue like a corrosive acid, exposing, too late, Matt Harper's sinister role in real life, as he sang half-hidden behind Goliath—the murderer I should have recognized in time. The songs sneak up on me as I stand absentmindedly at the sink washing dishes, or while I work my shampoo into a white lather in the shower. They're often wordless, just a scattering of notes, fragments of what I should have assembled and made whole from that fractured performance that will keep on repeating. Recently, I caught myself humming several bars of the score with a casualness that stunned me as I realized the context and stopped. I've wondered if the songs haunt Matt, too, if he ever thinks about the distant musical or replays our old roles, if the face of a Philistine giant mocks him from his cell's small mirror. I do know that, more than once, I've glimpsed a red-haired girl in my own bathroom mirror as I splash water on my face and blot my cheeks with a washcloth. She often lingers, even after I shut off the light.

EPITHALAMIUM WITH SKUNK PIGS

In sixteenth-century Europe, certain recipes for poison weren't complete without fat dribbled from the corpse of a redheaded man. Red, the rarest hair color, sprouts from only two percent of the world's scalps. Many of art and literature's most famous redheads include a host of untrustworthy biblical rogues: Lilith, Cain, Judas, the serpentine temptress painted on the domed sky of Michelangelo's Sistine Chapel. Even Eve's brunette locks sizzle to crimson after Adam bites the apple. One of my favorite notorious redheads is the witch queen of Arthurian legend, Morgan le Fay, who rules the enchanted Isle of Avalon. On Avalon, people live to be a hundred years old, or more, and the island's magical forests and fields provide apples, grapes, and grain without the inhabitants having to lift one finger in labor. The word Avalon comes from the Welch *afal*, meaning "apple."

It was on the mythic isle of apples that the Lady of the Lake, the high priestess of Avalon, presented King Arthur with the sword

Excalibur. In the legend, after Arthur receives a mortal wound during his fight with Mordred in the Battle of Camlann, the king sets sail for Avalon, with Morgan, in a black boat, hoping his half-sister might heal him. Some versions of the story suggest that Arthur died on the island, while others say he waits there to reclaim the throne of Britain someday. Yet the location of the Isle of Avalon remains mysterious; it's rumored to appear and disappear in the mists, forever shifting its location. Here, in Southern California, I've stood on the Venice Pier, near the psychedelic Sikh on rollerblades and a silver-haired ukulele player, and watched Catalina Island appear in the vaporous blue distance, then recede into the white sea fog.

. . . .

California's Avalon is a tiny seaside city, on the island of Catalina, whose pastel houses and wide-balconied hotels slope up the cove in a bright shuffle of tangerine, rose, and cornflower. Naming a city off the coast of Los Angeles after an enchanted isle may be one way to locate a myth. The act gives latitude and longitude to that longed-for place of magic apple trees, where one might enter a forest in which a fairy can heal a mortal wound.

. . . .

I eloped in ripped jeans, sandals, and a shirt of ivory lace, standing on the cliff edge of a dirt-covered stagecoach turnabout, in the mountains above Avalon. The ceremony's officiate, Anni, and her husband drove my husband-to-be, David, and me up the island's mountain roads in their shuddery, cherry-red Volkswagen bus. Watching Anni's dyed-orange hair flap in the wind from the cracked window made me recall a phrase from Norman Dubie's poem "*Ars Poetica*" in which the jilted, strawberry-blond muse has hair "[t]hat second chaste coat of red on the pomegranate." In the poem, a man tricks a woman—a worker from a nearby cigarette factory who's missing her left thumb—into stripping off her clothes. He then swims off with the bundle into the night surf, leaving her nude and alone on the beach as a joke. "Dubie's saying," my poetry teacher, Lee, had explained, "*Don't fuck with the muse.*"

The stagecoach turnabout in Avalon was flanked in ancient, gauzy-barked eucalyptus and a hip-high cedar fence. In the nineteenth century, the loop allowed a bulky coach to change direction with ease, so the horses wouldn't stumble trying to turn around on the narrow path and send everyone over the cliff. As David and I stepped from the van, menthol oil wafted from the trees' sage-green leaves. I can't smell the air around a eucalyptus without conjuring the scent of the cigarettes I smoked in high school— the mentholated Newports I'd suck down between lunch and gym class in the graffitied bathroom stalls. Once, after reading Plath's "Lady Lazarus" in my tenth-grade creative writing class, I scrawled the poem's final tercet in Wite-Out over the olive-colored wall: "Out of the ash / I rise with my red hair / And I eat men like air." The air hung sharp with menthol vapors on the day I married, and there in the trees wavered a line of pale girls exhaling their time-warped incense of smoke.

. . . .

In ninth grade, I'd sometimes play the Cigarette Game with my friend Laura, who drew black tears in the corners of her eyes with liquid liner and who would soon drop out of school due to her pregnancy. We'd sit on my front stoop, drop a lit Newport or Camel, lengthwise, between our forearms, and press our flesh together so the hot pinch of the cherry singed both of our skins. The first person to jerk away from the burn lost, though both of us would share a matching set of nine dime-sized scars. Alone, I once sat cross-legged on my carpet and heated the bottom loop of a steel coat hanger with my lighter, branding my own left bicep: three inch-long parallel burns now faded to white and flecked with maple-colored freckles split along the rippled scar tissue into the strange Vs of birds' feet.

After Laura and I painted a nightmarish mural of bloody handprints and anarchy symbols—using our actual blood—across one of my bedroom walls, which made my mother cry, my parents checked me into the adolescent wing of Dominion Hospital, a mental health facility in suburban Falls Church, where I met other high school girls from northern Virginia with problems more serious than my own. My roommate Pradeepa told me, as we sat facing each other on our parallel twin beds, that after her boyfriend had broken up with her, she'd climbed into her bathtub at home, pulled a plastic grocery sack over her head, then cinched and tied the handles beneath her chin. Her older brother had heard her crying and yanked the bathroom door off its hinges to reach her. Another girl, Sarah, looked like an athletic freshman volleyball player in her baggy T-shirt and gym shorts until she stood up to reveal her skeletal legs, bony and disproportionate as a foal's. Allison, a quiet fifteen-year-old with six-inch vertical scars running up her wrists, rose in the middle of lunch one day, snapped her plastic spork in half to make a blade, and started carving at her left forearm as other patients began to gasp and shriek. Each night a nurse on the late shift would do "bed checks" every half hour, opening the door to peer inside, throwing a narrow slice of light into the room.

. . . .

In *A Natural History of the Senses* Diane Ackerman notes that migrating monarch butterflies prefer to rest in coastal eucalyptus groves because the pungent oil helps keep predatory insects and blue jays at bay. This way, the butterflies sleep within a kind of fragrant force field.

. . . .

Two months before we eloped, David and I lay in bed with the windows open. The scents from the night garden sifted through our screens: the neighbor's white-starred hedge of jasmine, the raw olive-smell of the beach fog, the sweet pools of condensation on the coral tips of the finger mound—that bizarre, Martian-like succulent. I was thinking about the dream David had had a couple of weeks earlier: we flew to Rome to get married and rented a room at the end of a crimson-carpeted marble staircase, in a hotel just off the Piazza di Spagna. In the dream, getting a marriage license became a Kafka-level bureaucratic hassle. David would run to and from our hotel, up and down the staircase, with a stack of paperwork, only to discover that each time, upon arrival, we were missing a form. "Oh, yeah?" I'd said. I said nothing else, but each night, for two weeks, I went to sleep smiling. "You know your dream about Rome?" I finally asked as we lay in bed that night, listening to the neighbor drag her trashcan to the curb. "Ever think about doing that kind of thing in real life?"

. . . .

A year after my hospitalization, I found ways to escape, through literature, my life in suburban Fairfax, Virginia—its beige, 1970s ranch houses and pruned sugar maples in each yard. I read fantasy books about the taboo love affair between Robin Hood and Maid Marian, the heroic adventures of hobbits and elves, and the fantastical legends of Merlin, Queen Guinevere, and King Arthur. I taped a map of Tolkien's Middle Earth to my bedroom wall, wrinkling and staining the paper with green tea to make the drawing of the realm seem more aged, more credibly a relic. I thought wearing velvet dresses with princess sleeves would seem too conspicuously sentimental, so I wore royal blue crushed-velvet bell-bottoms with peasant blouses to feel more fantasy maiden than suburban teen. I even managed to convince my parents to buy me a twenty-two-string Celtic lap harp, on which I learned to pluck the ballad "Scarborough Fair" and the theme song from Franco Zeffirelli's 1968 adaptation of *Romeo and Juliet*, "A Time for Us." Sometimes I'd sit on a log in the backyard, under a wild dogwood, even though the burls made for a less-than-magical cushion. Once a little boy crept across the woods and spied on my practicing.

. . . .

Before I married David, I lived for nearly seven years in the company of one red-bearded man, three upright basses, one electric bass, two fiddles, numerous acoustic and electric guitars, a banjo, two full-sized keyboards, a ukulele, a mandolin, a theremin, a singing saw, and a kazoo-like instrument of my then boyfriend's invention called the "dildophone," which involved a silicone dildo banded by its beige root—in imitation of a trombone's brass slide—to the narrow end of a yellow kitchen funnel. This was the richly textured atmosphere of the longest relationship I've had during my adult life—my time with Carrick, the warm and gregarious musician from Appalachia with whom I lived for three years in Richmond, Virginia, and for another three and a half in Houston, Texas. In many ways, Carrick and I complemented each other—his goofy spontaneity to my obsessive focus, his center-stage gusto to my quiet reserve—although our childish arguments seemed to arise from similarly volatile temperaments. After years of bellowing at each other across the house, throwing books or cushions, and slamming doors, we were used to the chaos. But perhaps due to the fact of our longevity, the dynamic didn't feel extreme. Recently, as I lay in bed reading, it wasn't any of our numerous habitual activities—the bayou hikes, the nights with wine under our live oak, the fights about Carrick giving up his bands to move to Houston with me—that I recalled. It was our visit, early in the relationship, to an art exhibition in DC that re-created, in three dimensions, famous paintings by Vincent van Gogh. We'd waited until other museum guests emptied out of the life-sized *Bedroom in Arles* and then stepped into the simulated depths of the eggshell-blue and yellow room crowded with pale maple furniture. Because of the torqued perspective, van Gogh's trapezoidal hardwood floor sloped up toward the far wall, and the ceiling slanted down like an attic's, until we had to lower our heads, like Lewis Carroll's enlarged Alice. For a moment, Carrick and I sat on the bed in the corner, grinning and briefly magical figures, next to a folded red blanket.

. . . .

At various times in my life, I've been told I could pass for one of those red-haired maidens found in paintings by the Pre-Raphaelites, a circumstance that both amuses and embarrasses me. Once it was a man buying mulch when I worked as a cashier in the garden section of Lowe's hardware shop. I'd been leaning on a grey stone display fountain tiered in blue rows of potted delphinium. Once it was a girl tripping on a headful of acid, who spun in circles with Carrick and me as we danced at a Flaming Lips concert in Norfolk. Most recently, it was Susan, a friend of David's, who sent me an e-mail after she saw the wedding photograph in which David and

I make peace signs with our right hands as we stand in front of Anni's Volkswagen, my bouquet of sunflowers jammed in the bus's windshield wipers. "Love the fact that you chose Avalon—the place of immortality—for your wedding," Susan wrote. "And you, starring as Morgan le Fay . . . check out the Pre-Raphaelite painting of her by Frederick Sandys. In it, Morgan has hair astonishingly like yours! (Though she's wearing a bit more clothing . . . most of it not for you, but the leopard skin might make a great sarong.)"

. . . .

Sandys—a debt-ridden and never popular painter—lived for a time in Chelsea with one of the founders of the Pre-Raphaelite Brotherhood, Dante Gabriel Rossetti, who admired the exacting, sensual lines and somber beauty of Sandys's works. Many women obsess Sandys's canvases, particularly mythology's *femmes fatales*: Helen of Troy, Morgan le Fay, Medea, and the Arthurian temptress Vivien, who seduces Merlin to discover his secrets. Many women, too, populate Sandys's love life: Georgiana Creed, his first wife; Keomi Gray, who modeled for many of his paintings; and Mary Emma Jones, a young actress with whom he had nine children.

In Sandys's *Morgan le Fay; Queen of Avalon*, Morgan stands, gesticulant in a flowing emerald gown draped in leopard skin and golden fabric. She wears a crimson-and-lavender cape in a room crowded with red tapestries and carved wooden knickknacks and alchemic objects. An open book and a scroll lie on the floor at her feet. Instead of the omnipotent satisfaction or manic self-regard of a witch caught mid-spell, there's a melancholic intensity to Morgan's torqued lips and downcast eyes. It's as if her incantation is fraught with desperation. Maybe she strives to close the wound of her half-brother Arthur. Maybe the king's fate depends on the magic of her words.

. . . .

I tried to come up with some magical words of my own to read during the elopement ceremony. I began writing a poem for David to celebrate our union, my first epithalamium. In the poem, a newlywed couple sits on a seaside balcony, sharing an heirloom tomato. I typed the title, "Wedding Night: We Share an Heirloom Tomato on Our Hotel Balcony Overlooking the Ocean," which quickly took an ominous swerve: "Wedding Night: We Share an Heirloom Tomato on Our Hotel Balcony Overlooking the Ocean in Which Natalie Wood Drowned." The island's dark history had slipped into my would-be love poem.

On November 29, 1981, the actress Natalie Wood slipped from a yacht anchored off the shores of Catalina and drowned. She'd been drinking wine all evening with her husband Robert Wagner and the actor Christopher Walken, her costar in the in-progress sci-fi film *Brainstorm*. Allegedly, after Walken suggested that Wood spend more time starring in films and less time caring for her two young children, Wagner smashed a wine bottle on the table, causing Wood to flee to the cabin below. When Wood's body was discovered the next day floating in the Pacific, she was wearing a down jacket over her nightgown, and socks. The heaviness of her wet clothes must've dragged her under. And the coroner found on the side of the yacht's rubber dinghy a series of scratch marks. She may have heard the loose dinghy banging against the side of the boat, stooped to tighten the rope, and slipped on the swim step. In my poem, the speaker thinks she sees a phantom: Wood's briny scratches emerge in the tomato skin's salty pleats. She imagines the fruit she shares with her husband must have sprouted from an heirloom seed that washed ashore, decades ago, from the yacht—that the actress must've placed a gelatinous green wafer of tomato on her tongue sometime before she rolled into the water. "I'll never be able to read this damn poem at my wedding," I thought.

. . . .

Instead of my epithalamium-turned-elegy, I selected a passage from Rainer Maria Rilke's letter to Emanuel von Bodman, written in 1901:

> It is a question in marriage, to my feeling, not of creating a quick community of spirit by tearing down and destroying all boundaries, but rather a good marriage is that in which each appoints to the other guardian of his solitude, and shows him this confidence, the greatest in his power to bestow. A "togetherness" between two people is an impossibility, and where it seems, nevertheless, to exist, it is a narrowing, a reciprocal agreement which robs either one party or both of his fullest freedom and development. But, once the realization is accepted that even between the closest human beings infinite distances continue to exist, a wonderful living side by side can grow up, if they succeed in loving the distance between them, which makes it possible for each to see the other whole and against a wide sky!

When Rilke wrote, at the turn of the century, about the importance of lovers guarding one another's solitude, stagecoaches still roamed the back roads above Avalon. As David and I clattered in Anni's van along the winding dirt paths of the island's menthol-saturated interior, we decided that the florist had wrapped my sun-flower bouquet too tightly in white ribbon ("Like an amputee's stump," David joked), and we began to unwind the stems. The ribbon grew longer and more diaphanous. We retied the bow into something freer, more appealingly askew.

. . . .

I'd met David at a literary conference on the work of the late poet Larry Levis, at Virginia Commonwealth University. Lee had invited both of us to Richmond for the event: I was to participate in a panel at my alma mater and present a paper on Levis's work, and David was scheduled to give a poetry reading; he'd been one of Levis's closest friends, first in Fresno and then in Iowa City, eventually editing several of Levis's posthumous collections. At the time, I was still living with Carrick in Houston as I completed the final semester of my PhD, both of us miserable yet invested in our hope that moving back to Virginia would somehow solve all of our problems. Nevertheless, I found myself meeting David for drinks at the bar of the Jefferson, Richmond's grandest old hotel. I'd admired David's poetry since I was an MFA student and had even sent him a copy of my first book of poems. We'd exchanged friendly e-mails for over a year. "It's just a drink," I'd shrugged to myself, glancing down at my watch, then up at the marble columns, stained-glass windows, and gold-leafed ceilings. I'd even told Carrick in advance about my cocktail plans. As I waited for David to appear, I flipped through a pamphlet about the fountains in the Jefferson's Palm Court, once home to a small population of tame alligators during the Jazz Age, including a creature named Old Pompey. One night, an alligator had allegedly slithered from its marble pool and into the hotel library, where an elderly woman who'd been sipping sherry as she browsed through books mistook the creature for a leather footstool, crossing her ankles over the reptile's cool back. When the "footstool" began to crawl, the woman screamed and fled from the room. Witnesses were divided about whether or not to believe her, as the alligator had vanished, and she vowed never to drink sherry again. As I sipped my amber Bellini, I peered over the lips of the champagne flute as a man with a trim silver beard and a black leather jacket appeared in the doorway of the Jefferson's bar, the mahogany walls shimmering from the tea lights.

. . . .

As we drew near the wedding site, Anni began to tell us about the island's javelina infestation. Ten years earlier, Catalina had teemed with an overpopulation of bristly, brown, dwarf-hippo-shaped "skunk pigs" and so local officials contracted a team of Midwestern hunters to fly in and thin the herds with machine gun fire. "I think Anni's trying to outdo my epithalamium," I whispered to David. Anni continued, recalling how the whole island reeked for weeks from the shot and rotting carcasses that stacked the hillsides. She'd drive to work, leading couples to various scenic island peaks to say their vows, and packs of black-eyed orphaned javelina would stampede from the groves, crossing the path of the van. Swarms of yellow jackets soon rose from the decaying meat, so the islanders then faced a winged plague. The javelina hunters had to switch from shooting Avalon's skunk pigs to poisoning insect nests with soap.

Although most brides likely would've been furious to receive such a gruesome, corpse-strewn send-off into holy matrimony, I loved the story. It gave texture and depth to an otherwise stilted scene: two couples—formerly strangers—in a van filled with beach-mart champagne; my mangled sunflowers; my feeling ridiculous about booming Rilkean proclamations from a seaside cliff. If javelina feel threatened, I learned, they rub their tusks together to create a rough, chattering sound. I imagined Avalon's forests must have echoed so profoundly that the whole island couldn't sleep, even King Arthur. I imagined the dark seed of the heirloom tomato stretched back to an ancestor once plucked up by Natalie Wood, linking all of us in its fine, slow helix.

As the van stopped at the stagecoach turnabout and I slid open the door, I imagined Morgan le Fay finally finding the right words as she whispered over the wound, and the wound as it healed and shut.

THE GUINEVERES

My mother's always marveled at Ted Bundy's charisma, his trick with the fake injuries, his voluminous hairdo. Throughout my childhood she'd recite the serial killer's murderous steps like a mantra—the arm sling, the dropped stack of books, the women Bundy shoved into his white Volkswagen Beetle. "Don't ever get into a stranger's car," she warned my younger sister and me. At the dinner table, she'd describe Trotsky's death by ice pick to his skull—a topic often triggered when my sister, my father, and I thrust our miniature yellow corncob handles into either side of the grilled and buttered ears. She'd tell the tale in a hushed tone, as if the Marxist's assassination were her own personal gossip. I enjoyed how the weapon in the story morphed from ice pick to splitting ax to bread knife, depending on my mother's dining utensil. Another frequent cameo in my mother's dinnertime anecdotes was Travis, the pet chimpanzee who went berserk one day at his home in Connecticut and gnawed off a woman's face. But the story my mother repeated with particular

urgency was Rosie's: the ten-year-old kidnapped from our neighborhood in 1989, whose smothered body was discovered under
the branches of a pine. My mother told us about Rosie's murder so
often that, as I walked home from school one afternoon in seventh
grade and a middle-aged Asian American couple pulled over in their
van, my stomach seized up. As the woman in the passenger's seat
unfolded a map and asked me about the location of Zion Road, I
sprinted off, my green backpack flapping against my spine. I was
determined not to let that pair of expertly disguised serial killers
throttle me and drop my body in the nearby creek.

Growing up, the macabre character of my mother's anecdotes
didn't strike me as unusual. I listened to their dark morals the same
way I received the fairy tales she'd read to my little sister and me: rapt
and at a safe distance. I imagined other people's mothers told similar
sorts of cautionary tales meant to encourage children to be vigilant:
*Don't go into the woods by yourself. Don't knock on a stranger's door and
get shoved into an oven.* In one moment, she'd recount how Hans
Christian Andersen's Little Mermaid's fishtail split into human legs,
and that every step the transformed creature took felt like "walking
on knives." In another, she'd describe the dexterous feet of the armless thalidomide girl who attended her family's Episcopalian church,
in Jackson, and who could grip, at picnics, a slice of watermelon
between her toes. If at bedtime my mother planned to read to us
from a book in which bloodthirsty Norwegian cave trolls threatened
to bite Peer Gynt's bottom or gouge out his eyes, then bringing up
the Manson murders over fried chicken earlier that night seemed
"on message": *The world is a dangerous place. There's a randomness to
suffering and violence. I love you, but no one is safe.*

I don't remember when my sister and I began referring to
my mother's most frequently repeated tales as "Mom's Greatest
Hits." I think I was an undergraduate in art school, so it must've

been when I was around nineteen and Rebecca was a junior in high school. I realized from my freshman roommate's incredulous reactions that my mother's stories might be peculiar: "She said *what*? So that's where you get it from!" Somehow, I'd been able to reconcile my mother's sunny, preternatural innocence and Southern charm with her interest in the most extreme or savage regions of human experience. On one side of the innocence/experience spectrum, she grew up a sheltered, middle-class Southern belle in Jackson, Mississippi: the Baby Boomer favorite daughter of a prominent psychiatrist and a gracious nurse. My mother was a longtime Girl Scout; attended a small women's college in Columbus; taught fourth grade for several years before marrying my father; moved overseas and raised two children; and since the mid-nineties she's worked two jobs as a cashier at JCPenney and a cheerful teacher's aide to first-grade students at a suburban Virginia elementary school. Although I laughed when she confessed she didn't know the meaning of the word "turd" until the summer after her first year of college (one of her father's patients gave her the nickname when she worked at his hospital for a summer as a psychiatric aide), I wasn't at all surprised. On the other side of the innocence/experience divide lie the monstrous or tragic figures that populate her "Greatest Hits": Trotsky, Bundy, Rosie, Manson, the face-eating chimpanzee Travis. I've come to wonder whether the family dinner table conjures for my mother the crackling bonfires around which she sat during those six consecutive summers at Camp Wahi, first as a Girl Scout camper and then as a counselor telling "Bluebeard" to an audience of enthralled little girls.

. . . .

Part of my mother's matter-of-fact attitude toward bizarre subjects likely comes from her own parents: their blend of clinical directness and their fondness for family history. My mother's parents—native Texans—met just after World War II, at the University of Texas Medical Branch, in Galveston, where my grandmother Dorothy Bowman worked as a nurse and where my grandfather Lisburn Clarence Hanes ("L. C.") was enrolled in medical school. My grandparents often talked shop at the dinner table. They'd casually offer my mother and her younger sister Becky an anecdotal buffet of abnormalities, injuries, and illnesses as they passed the fried chicken. One story that fascinated my mother involved a grotesque discovery: My grandmother began her shift as a night supervisor and noticed that a boy born earlier that day wouldn't stop crying. She checked the chart, on which a nurse from the earlier shift had recorded taking his temperature, which was done, in the mid-1940s, with a rectal thermometer. As my grandmother unwrapped the baby's diaper and prepared to take his temperature, she discovered that the other nurse had lied on the chart. The child had been born without an anus—his buttocks were sealed completely shut, like the dimple in the side of an heirloom tomato. The image of my grandmother turning the newborn over in her hands to discover the missing feature shocked my mother, who retold the story to her own children around the supper table.

. . . .

To make sure we'd be able to escape from murderers or molesters if we were snatched while walking home from Oak View Elementary, my mother made Rebecca and me practice our lines and simulate being kidnapped as we stood side by side on the yellow tiles of our kitchen floor. "What do you say when he pulls into a gas station," our mother asked, "or if he takes you into a convenience store?" "This man is not my father!" we shouted, giggling and nudging each other. "I've been kidnapped! Call the police!" We were eager to report to our mother our suspicions about the red-mustached man who lived down the block. He'd drag his green bags of yard waste to the curb, which, when viewed through binoculars pressed through a juniper hedge, resembled sacks filled with dismembered bodies. Rebecca and I lay in the grass, propped on our elbows, and scribbled in our spiral notebooks the outlines of elbows and feet that we imagined jutted incriminatingly from the plastic lawn bags. "Is that a nose?" Rebecca asked, hopefully. "Maybe a big toe?" "A nose. Definitely a nose," I said, raising the field glasses to my eyes.

. . . .

My grandfather was careful not to divulge privileged information about his psychiatric patients, though he'd readily share with his family other aspects of his medical experience. His hulking, leather-bound *Encyclopedia of Infectious Diseases and Medical Anomalies* doubled as bedtime reading for my mother, who flipped, fascinated, through photographs, drawings, and descriptions of tumors, boils, skull fractures, and gargantuan limbs of patients swollen from elephantiasis. Although he worked in his middle age toward advancing integration policies, in Jackson, during the civil rights movement (prompting the Ku Klux Klan to plant a wooden cross in his front yard and set it on fire), he confessed his participation in a shameful tradition among the doctors at the hospital in Galveston. Approximately once a year, a young African American woman gave birth at the facility. Each time, she'd ask one of the residents to name her new child. The doctors conspired with one another to name each baby after a halogen element on the periodic table, which were, in their opinion, the most euphonic. I've wondered about that family of siblings who grew up along the Gulf Coast with the names Fluorine, Chlorine, Bromine, Iodine (pronounced

"Eye-oh-deen"), and Astatine. My grandfather—haunted by his complicity—shook his head in chagrin at the tale's insidious racism and classist condescension. Perhaps he—a lay reader who served the sacramental wine every Sunday at his Episcopalian church—repeated the story to his wife and children in the hopes that someone might eventually absolve him.

Perhaps he was reminded of his own unusual first name, Lisburn—the name of that small town in Northern Ireland he'd never seen. Those syllables must have hissed, rare and sibilant, as they echoed through the dusty air among the Bobs, Bills, and Butches of his childhood in a tiny West Texas town called Wink. Perhaps the Halogen Daughters learned to abbreviate their wayward names the way my grandfather had, as he whittled his down to its initials: the simple L. C. Maybe he sipped his malt whiskey at the dinner table, implicated, as my mother and her little sister sat to his right and left, letting the reticent vowels of the elements roll off their tongues. Maybe he—a scientist—imagined the language gaining electrons as it grew increasingly reactive. As if the words, repeating, would attack all inert matter in the room.

. . . .

My mother's favorite stories to tell around Girl Scout bonfires at Camp Wahi (which was named using abbreviations of the first half of each word in "Water Hill" and located just outside of Brandon, Mississippi) were the marital horror story "Bluebeard," by Charles Perrault, and the violent fairy tale about sibling rivalry, "One-Eye, Two-Eyes, and Three-Eyes," recounted by the Brothers Grimm. In addition to serving as a counselor one year, my mother became a song leader as a teenage camper. She often picked musical rounds in which the girls, divided into groups, sang the same melody, beginning the song at different times so their voices layered to create a dense texture woven with harmonies and echoes, as in "*Frère Jacques*" or "Hear the Lively Song." She especially loved the French round "*Le Carillon de Vendôme*" for the way its sonorous vowels sounded like the rich pealing of cathedral bells. Her favorite round was a humorous onomatopoeic composition in which the girls simultaneously spoke, rather than sung, three phrases. The first group repeated: "potatoes, potatoes, potatoes"; the second: "tomatoes, tomatoes, tomatoes"; and the third: "fried bacon, fried bacon, fried bacon." As the campers chanted, their words seemed to free themselves from their meanings and—transformed—morphed into the vibrant, nocturnal chorus of an echoing frog pond.

....

It's also possible my mother repeats her stories due to the gothic nature of her early childhood. From ages four through six she lived with her parents and little sister Becky in a brick house on the grounds of Austin State Hospital while my grandfather completed his residency, from 1950 to 1952. The psychiatric hospital, formerly called the Texas State Lunatic Asylum, stretched in a series of low brick buildings and was surrounded by a high cyclone fence. In a gravel cul-de-sac just outside of the chain link stood four identical one story houses provided by the hospital to medical residents and their families: two structures on either side of the road. The cul-de-sac dead-ended at the edge of a wide cornfield, walling off the odd, miniature suburb and providing a sort of forest in which the children could play. And as if to reinforce the mirror image, half the houses held couples with children and the other half without. The Legget family had three children; the two oldest were Becky's and my mother's exact ages. And coincidentally, my mother and her neighborhood playmate also shared the same name: Cindy.

The two Cindys like to crawl into the wooden doghouse belonging to Duchess, my mother's fat, ice cream–loving dachshund, and play tea party using Cindy Legget's fluted white china set with the mock-silver spoons. From where the girls sat in the backyard doghouse sipping tap water from their cups, their ladylike pinkie fingers sticking straight out, they could hear periodic hoots and wails washing downwind from the nearby women's ward. At one point, a patient escaped from the men's ward and wandered loose through the hospital grounds, sending the whole place into lockdown. My grandparents forbade my mother and Becky from playing in the cornfield, saying that the confused patient could be crouched between the tall stalks, waiting to pull them in. When I asked my mother if the staff ever caught the escaped patient, she paused and said she didn't know. "How can you not know?" I asked. "I was four," she said, shrugging. She was finally allowed back into the thicket of stalks, listening for rattlesnakes as she shimmied her way through the corn, keeping her house safely within sight.

One night, after my grandparents had left for a dinner party in town, my mother and Becky went to bed and their babysitter, sixteen-year-old Aunt Jeannette (their father's baby sister), sat in the living room, reading. Several hours later, while the kids slept, a man broke into the house, tied Jeannette up with panty hose he found in the master bedroom, and rifled through my grandmother's jewelry box. He managed to slip out the back door when he heard my grandparents pull into the driveway. As they entered the house, Jeannette jerked her head in the direction of the fleeing burglar, and my grandfather raced toward the door as my grandmother darted down the hall to the children's room.

Soon, Becky and my mother sat on a pink quilt my grandmother had spread across the Leggets' front yard as the manhunt began. My mother recalls a posse of men scouring the hospital grounds as they carried shotguns against their shoulders—one of the gunslinging volunteers scuttling around shirtless, in his underwear. She kept hearing the word "burglar" echoing from the men's mouths—a word she didn't yet know. Her "burglar," she imagined, must be a monster made from fistfuls of hamburger meat, who prowled the neighborhood in his raw, pink flesh, looking for little girls to eat.

My own favorite monster from childhood was the Troll King from "Peer Gynt," who makes the lazy, ragamuffin farmer, Peer, drink sour pig's mead and attach a green tail to his bottom to prove he's prepared to marry the troll princess. In my edition of the fairy tale, the illustrator, Paul Bonner, had given the Troll King wild white hair and a gourd-shaped nose that shone like greenish brass. My mother would read the part where the Troll King calls for Peer's death—after the insolent Norwegian mocks the king's daughter's harp playing—with an imperial roar: "Dash him to bits upon the rocks!" She'd pitch her voice higher to conjure the petulant, adolescent troll chorus, giddily clamoring for Peer's blood: "May we not torment him first, Your Majesty?"

. . . .

"Cindy Hanes is a most attractive young lady of 23, who is currently appearing at the Jackson Little Theatre in their production of 'Harvey,'" writes Loy Moncrief, a local actor and business manager for the Theater Center, in a clipping from the *Jackson Daily News*, which my grandmother had saved and pasted into a scrapbook. Moncrief's article about my mother's role as a nurse in Mary Chase's comedy of errors, *Harvey*, simmers with a certain genteel, period-style sexism that both amuses me and makes me squirm. In the article "Dumb, Beautiful Nurse In 'Harvey' Only Half Typecast" (August 28, 1970), Moncrief writes: "In the role of Miss Kelley she is the, [*sic*] 'dum [*sic*] but beautiful' nurse at Chumley's Rest (a psychiatric treatment center). Miss Hanes is certainly beautiful, but not in the least dumb, though she is certainly adept at appearing so on stage." In the accompanying photograph my glamorous, dark-haired mother wears a crisp white nurse's uniform and pointed cap as she grips the elbow of Cliff Bingham, the middle-aged actor who starred as Elwood P. Dowd, the play's main character who halluci-nates a six-foot-tall rabbit named Harvey. She's made her radiant, canny smile appear dopey and a bit dazed, and she tilts her head coyly toward Bingham.

During one performance of *Harvey*, my mother recalls that the actor (a local TV weatherman) who played the doctor at the sani-tarium to which Elwood gets committed suddenly froze mid-scene, forgetting his lines—he "went up," as theater folks say—and she had to improvise some dialogue in order to keep the story going.

Moncrief summarizes my mother's background as follows:

> Cindy is not a native Mississippian. She was born in Galveston, Texas. She moved around quite a bit in her early childhood. Her family lived in Texas, Cali-fornia and Louisiana until the time she was in the seventh grade. At that point her Father [*sic*] (who is a prominent psychiatrist in Jackson) moved the family to Jackson, because he wanted to work on the newly forming psychiatric department at the University Medical Center.

He also mentions that during her senior year at Mississippi State College for Women, my mother was elected president of her school's chapter of the Alpha Psi Omega Honorary Dramatics Fra-ternity, and lists several of her appearances in collegiate and community theater productions: "'J.B.,' 'Something Unspoken,' 'Alice in Wonderland,' 'The Miracle Worker,' 'First Lady,' 'Lilliom,' and 'The Time of the Cuckoo,' among others." She's told me that her favorite roles were the drunken Italian maid, Giovanna, in Arthur Laurents's *The Time of the Cuckoo*, for which she trained with an Italian language coach and received a Sammy Award for Best Cameo Actress, and the elusive White Rabbit in *Alice in Wonderland*. My mother's first community theater role, while she was still in high school, was a small part as a young blind girl in William Gibson's *The Miracle Worker* in which her own father (a bearded, bespectacled doctor) played the doctor (bearded, bespectacled) who delivers the blind and deaf infant Helen Keller. His one line: "She'll live."

"She loves singing as well as acting," Moncrief notes of my mother. He then quotes her directly: "'My singing career was cut short when I had a small malignancy removed from my throat a couple of years ago. But my voice is getting stronger and I'm regaining my confidence in it.'"

My mother had told me about her cancer. After her father noticed a lump on her throat and took her the next day to see the head of endocrinology at the University of Mississippi Medical Center, she was diagnosed, at twenty-two, with a malignant tumor on her thyroid gland. Surgeons removed sixty percent of her thyroid, along with a parathyroid gland and a lymph node. She'd never mentioned to me, however, the operation's effect on her voice or that she'd envisioned for herself a professional singing career.

. . . .

My mother played the role of folk singer in two different productions: Hewitt Griffin's *A Walk in the Forest* and Charles Aidman's musical adaptation of Edgar Lee Masters's *Spoon River Anthology*. In a photograph from another clipping my grandmother saved from the *Jackson Daily News* (January 19, 1971), my mother perches on a stool, as she sings and strums an acoustic guitar for her role in *A Walk in the Forest*. She looks like a sixties countercultural archetype: her long brown hair's flat-ironed and parted in the middle and she wears a white peasant blouse over a patchwork skirt. In *The Clarion-Ledger* (March 4, 1971), Jean Culbertson writes of my mother's performance in *Spoon River Anthology*: "Cindy Hanes's lingering voice has an especially memorable quality on this type of folk music." James Gordon, in the *Jackson Daily News*, describes *Spoon River* as "a panorama of human experience related by voices from the grave."

In addition to acting as a folk singer in plays, my mother was, for several years, an actual folk singer. In 1964 she began her freshman year at Mississippi State College for Women, in the small city of Columbus, where she and her best friend Donna—a fellow Girl Scout and veteran of Camp Wahi—decided to pledge a social club at "the W" called the Lancers, which they'd heard was populated with "good girls." Donna had told members of the Lancers' leadership that Cindy Hanes was a formidable storyteller around a Girl Scout campfire. While the Lancers asked one pledge to churn vanilla ice cream on the dining hall's screened-in back porch and required another to act out the phrase "give birth to a nation," they asked my mother to tell a story. My mother stood in front of the pledges and gave one of her theatrical performances of "Bluebeard." I've wondered if the roomful of Southern belles sitting cross-legged on the hardwood of the Great Hall reminded her of the crowded floor of Bluebeard's chamber.

In my mother's version of the tale, Bluebeard possessed the growling bass voice of an ogre, while his wife's long vowels sounded like those drawled by a naïve yet adaptive girl from Jackson. She lingered over the description of Fatima's discovery of Bluebeard's secret room, the one he'd forbidden his new bride from entering: the blood coagulated on the floor like canned pie cherries; the rows of dead women—his former wives—wrapped in sheets; the most recent victim still swinging from the chandelier, her toes swollen and blue. Even the bottom hems of the white curtains in Bluebeard's murder room were soaked with foot-long stains that spread up from the gory floor. The women clapped, roaring their approval, and elected my mother vice president of the Lancers and the social club's resident storyteller.

Because my mother and Donna—who roomed together in the dorm—often sat outside strumming the instruments they'd brought from home (my mom on acoustic guitar and Donna on baritone ukulele) and singing songs they'd learned together at Camp Wahi, the other Lancers encouraged them to form a folk band with another woman in the social club, Iva, who sang in an ethereal, clear soprano. The Lancers needed a regular band for entertainment at their events as well as the parties they often co-hosted with the Mississippi State University fraternity, Phi Tau, at which several Lancers had boyfriends. So my mother, Donna, and Iva formed a folk trio and called themselves the Guineveres, after Queen Guinevere of Arthurian legend. In the harmony Iva sang soprano, Donna alto, and my mother the melody, the latter two taking turns playing rhythm and lead on their instruments.

At Lancers' parties, the Guineveres played a range of songs, drawing from American roots music as well as more recent popular tunes: George Gershwin's haunting, jazzy "Summertime"; the African American spiritual "Michael, Row the Boat Ashore"; Lead Belly's bluesy downtuned "Bring Me a Little Water, Sylvie"; Peter, Paul, and Mary's whimsical "Puff, the Magic Dragon"; The Limeliters' political tune "Harry Pollitt"; the utopic Girl Scout campfire song "I Know a Place"; the eerie New Orleans ballad "The House of the Rising Sun." At one point, while my mother was rehearsing "The House of the Rising Sun" in a communal room in her dorm, a woman asked permission to record her singing. The woman wanted to send a tape to her boyfriend, who was fighting in Vietnam. Midway through the song, there's a verse that reminds me of my mother's cautionary tales:

> Oh mother, tell your children
> Not to do what I have done
> Spend your lives in sin and misery
> In the House of the Rising Sun

I've wondered about the young soldier in Vietnam who received the tape of my mother singing. I've tried to imagine her warm mezzo-soprano and simple, strummed chords echoing in the remote jungles. I've hoped he found comfort and beauty in her voice, and that he finally returned, alive, to Mississippi.

One song the Guineveres regularly performed, "The Little Land," by the folk and blues singer-songwriter Malvina Reynolds, warns of the harrowing spells of Irish leprechauns, who would work their Rip Van Winkle-esque magic on unsuspecting travelers. The lyrics remind me of the fairy tales my mother tells:

> When you're in the Little Land,
> They fill your hands with gold,
> You think you stay for a just a day,
> You come out bent and old.

. . . .

I remember the single summer day that bent and aged my mother. The day Rebecca ran down to the basement, where I was watching

TV, to tell me she could hear our mom calling for help but that she couldn't find her. Our dad was at work in DC. We climbed upstairs together—Rebecca was seven and I was ten. When we found our mother, she was sprawled on the garage floor and couldn't move. She'd stepped through a thin patch of drywall in the attic's floor and plunged to the concrete, breaking her spine. I called 911 and shrieked at the operator that I thought my mother had cracked her head open and was dying.

I don't have a clear sense of the months my mother spent in the hospital after the accident. I remember my godparents driving Rebecca and me to the pool, taking us camping by a lake, and giving us a video to watch while our mother was away in which three chipmunk sisters (relatives of Alvin, Simon, and Theodore) sing about missing their mother. "A friend and a teacher, always I need her. My mother, that's who I need," the little girl chipmunks sang.

After multiple surgeries, fused vertebrae, and steel screws that left her back permanently curved at forty-four, my mom was the one who needed a protector and a storyteller. I quit horseback riding. I quit the swim team. I quit piano. Although Rebecca wasn't old enough to understand why our mother was suddenly unavailable, why she'd shape-shifted from the ebullient facilitator of our lives into a groggy, horizontal specter, I knew the reason our family's dynamic had shifted. Our mother was now the vulnerable one, dazed from her constant pain and bound to the grey couch in the living room. For a year, my mother and I switched roles: I'd perch at her feet as she lay in her white turtle-shell-like back brace and tell her about the silver mine I believed I'd discovered in the black soil beneath the deck or my plans to make bamboo paintbrushes tipped in bristles from the severed squirrel's tail my father had found and saved for me while raking the hillside's leaves.

. . . .

In "The Little Land," the chorus goes:

> Dead leaves in your pockets,
> Oh, my enchanted, have a care!
> Run, run from the Little Folk
> Or you'll have dead leaves in your pockets
> And snowflakes in your hair.

I've tried not to picture the Vietnam soldier running through the jungle, his pockets filling with dead leaves as he falls. I've tried not to see the snowflakes gathering in my mother's once-dark hair.

. . . .

The summer before her sophomore year of college, my mother played in an unnamed folk quartet at the Sea Gun Sports Inn, in Rockport, the small coastal city known as "the Texas Riviera." The band's other members were my mother's Aunt Jeannette (nine years her senior) and two of Jeannette's friends: Denny, a laid-back local singer, and Mark, a brilliant minister's son who built early computer prototypes out of his garage. My mother played rhythm guitar, while Mark and Jeannette traded on lead. All four of them sang in harmony. Mostly they performed by the inn's poolside and then played another set on the *Whooping Crane*, the cocktail boat that took hotel guests for a slow jaunt at dusk around the bay.

My grandmother, who'd majored in Home Economics before attending nursing school, made a matching set of hippie shirts for the quartet: four vest-like burlap pullovers appliqued with flowers and finished at the collar with decorative leather laces. She also made my mother an elaborate grey chiffon gown for her musical performance at the college's "Miss W" pageant in which she dressed up as the wind. My mother sang Alan J. Lerner's and Frederick Loewe's show tune "They Call the Wind Mariah" from the Broadway musical *Paint Your Wagon* and, as she strummed her guitar, the draped lengths of fabric billowed and waved.

. . . .

Although my mother's thyroid cancer may have cut short her professional career as a folk singer, there've been no shortage of songs in our house. She taught Rebecca and me the haunting English round, "Rose, Rose, Rose, Rose," about a father urging his daughter toward marriage, which begins:

> Rose, Rose, Rose, Rose,
> Will I ever see thee wed?
> I will marry at thy will, Sire,
> At thy will.

A subsequent verse conflates the wedding ritual with a mossy funerary stone, the church bells tolling for both life changes, and the song suggests the Elizabethan maiden sees in the marriage union her own inevitable death:

> Ding dong, ding dong.
> Wedding bells on an April morn'.
> Carve my name on a moss covered stone,
> On a moss covered stone.

There's a quality of psychological darkness to so many of these folk songs—fraught with death and human suffering and beguiling or cruel magic spells—that I've always admired. I love them for their vivid imagery, charged diction, and stories of longing and mystery. In third grade, I remember wielding the Appalachian murder ballad "Tom Dooley" as a playground taunt to verbally assault my neighbor when she teased Rebecca for wearing glasses. I substituted the condemned murderer Tom Dooley's name with my neighbor Brie's and sang:

> Hang down your head, Brie Roddy
> Hang down your head and cry
> Hang down your head, Brie Roddy
> Poor girl, you're bound to die
> This time tomorrow
> Reckon where you'll be
> Down in some lonesome valley
> Hanging from a white oak tree

Brie, a gregarious tomboy with a knack for doodling cartoon cats, did in fact hang down her head and cry. As she sprinted off, I felt guilty, but I also felt the awful power of the song's dark story.

. . . .

John and Alan Lomax, the nomadic song-collecting father and son duo who were the most influential documentarians of American folk music during the twentieth century, describe in their preface to *Our Singing Country: Folk Songs and Ballads* the cultural importance of preserving the songs of ordinary American folk. "Most of these singers," write the Lomaxes:

> are poor people, farmers, laborers, convicts, old-age pensioners, relief workers, housewives, wandering guitar pickers. These are the people who still sing the work songs, the cowboy songs, the sea songs, the lumberjack songs, the bad-man ballads, and other

songs that have no occupation or special group to keep them alive. These are the people who are making new songs today. These are the people who go courting with their guitars, who make the music for their own dances, who make their own songs for their own religion. These are the story-tellers, because they are the people who are watching when things happen.

The Lomaxes traveled the US recording folk songs in the 1930s, creating, under the direction of Herbert Putnam, the Archive of American Folk Song in the Library of Congress. Popular awareness of this diverse and vibrant narrative tradition in American blues, folk, and country music culminated in the 1950s and '60s, with the release, by Folkways Records, of Harry Smith's groundbreaking compilation of folk songs, *Anthology of American Folk Music*, in 1952. At the time, the LP medium was still fairly new. Smith's six-album set directly led to the rediscovery (by singers such as John Cohen and Mike Seeger, of the New Lost City Ramblers, and by later artists such as Joan Baez, Bob Dylan, Jerry Garcia, and Dave Van Ronk) of performers previously known only to regional audiences.

It's not coincidental that the folk movement, with its potent narratives of human suffering, longing, and labor, began to coincide and coalesce with the civil rights movement. The union-organizing song "We Shall Overcome," written by Zilphia Hart and published by the folk singer and activist Pete Seeger in *People's Songs Bulletins*, in 1948, became the anthem of the civil rights movement when the folk musician, musicologist, and activist Guy Carawan taught the song to the members of the Student Nonviolent Coordinating Committee, in 1960. Although my mom sang "We Shall Overcome" at home, among her friends and family, she didn't dare perform it in public with the Guineveres. "That's not a song you would *ever* sing at a fraternity party in Mississippi," she told me. "I would never have performed that song in the South and kept my life." Her fear at first dismayed and even angered me. Then I recalled the murders, by the Ku Klux Klan, of the three civil rights activists, in Philadelphia, Mississippi, in 1964, two months before my mother began her freshman year at MSCW. The site of the shootings lay fewer than eighty-two miles from my mother's school, less than an hour and a half's drive down highways 82 and 45.

A year earlier, in August, 1963, Joan Baez famously led a crowd of over three hundred thousand people in singing "We Shall Overcome" at the Lincoln Memorial, during the March on Washington. And later, Dr. Martin Luther King Jr., during his final sermon delivered in Memphis, in March of 1968 (in which he declares, "the arc of the moral universe is long, but it bends towards justice"), recited the song's familiar refrain: "We shall overcome. We shall overcome. Deep in my heart I do believe we shall overcome."

Folk songs are not only able to enlarge the national conscience as they pass from one person to another, they often reveal the darkness and universality of intimate human suffering as well as the transformative power of the imagination. These are songs of a jealous girl pushing her sister into a stream to drown, in the English-turned-Appalachian ballad "Dreadful Wind and Rain"; of an African American woman named Dink who longs to sprout the wings of a dove to fly to her absent lover working in a levee camp upriver, in "Dink's Song"; of an anguished man who contemplates drowning himself in the river or overdosing on morphine because he can't get over his heartache, in Lead Belly's "Goodnight, Irene"; of the woman whose feet are so preposterously huge that she wears herring boxes for sandals and dies of a splinter, in the Gold Rush burlesque "Clementine." Of the American folk singers, the Lomaxes observe elsewhere in their preface: "These are the great laughers and the great liars, because they know that life is so much more ridiculous than anyone can ever hope to tell. These are the people who understand death, because it has been close to them all their lives."

. . . .

My mother's confessed that she'd never have thought to form a folk band on her own, that she played her guitar with Donna as recreation. It reminded her of singing with the girls around the campfire during all those years at Camp Wahi. She says she "fell into" the trio when the Lancers asked her to play with Donna and Iva. When I ask how they arrived at the name the Guineveres, my mother provides a straightforward answer: They played lots of old British songs and American folk ballads and the name sounded appropriately old-fashioned. They also attended a women's college. Fair enough. But I like to imagine their homage to Queen Guinevere—wife of King Arthur and mistress of Sir Lancelot—as a subversive and empowering, even a defiant, choice. Guinevere is our medieval rule-breaker. She's mythic: she's Eve or Pandora. She's epic: she's Helen of Troy. Her wild, taboo passion for the knight Lancelot creates the major narrative arc in the legend—Guinevere sets all the plot twists and tragedies in motion. What better way to defy the patriarchy (the deans, the Bluebeards, the Southern frat boys) than to pluralize her?

I'm certain that if I'd had a different sort of mother—one who wasn't fascinated by macabre stories and death-haunted songs—I wouldn't have grown up to become a writer. I'm certain I would never have learned the word *elephantiasis* before I knew the capital of Virginia. "What the people of a country do with the music they take over for themselves and the poems they take over for themselves," writes Archibald MacLeish in his introduction to the 1941 edition of the Lomaxes' second volume of American ballads and folk songs, "is to pass them along from hand to hand, from mouth to mouth, from one generation to the next, until they wear smooth in the shape the people—this particular people—is obliged to give them." I love the way the stories my mother passed down to me at the dinner table still spark and settle as if at the volatile edge of a bonfire. I love the way, repeating, they shape-shift, like the voices of young girls morphing into frog song in the dark, and how, through the years, I've learned to hear in these stories the echo of my own voice.

STRANGE MERCHANTS

My father was once mistaken for a hit man. A tweed-wearing, mustached former Peace Corps volunteer, he appears the most unlikely assassin. In 1977, my thirty-four-year-old father lived with my mother in Ottawa. He worked as a consultant for the health sciences division of the International Development Research Centre. On his way back from a business trip to La Paz, Bolivia, where he scouted rural areas as possible loci for sanitation projects, my father stopped in front of a leather goods store in the middle of El Alto International Airport. In the shop's display window hung a dark brown leather trench coat, with maroon undertones, selling for the equivalent of a hundred and fifty US dollars. My father imagined himself in the trench coat, braced against the glacial Ottawan wind chill that drove his neighbor to hang herself with a clothesline the week before his trip.

At the counter stood a man in his mid-sixties, with fraying white hair and a wide speckled forehead. My father smiled and pointed to the display jacket, asking, in Spanish, if he might try it on. The man said he was welcome to and began to move from behind the cash register. My father, a linguaphile who'd lived in Berlin, Hamburg, Bavaria, and Peine, noticed the man spoke Spanish with a thick German accent. *"Das Leben is wie ein Kinderhemd, Kurz und beschissen!"* my father joked, recalling a well-known German aphorism. ("Life is like a child's shirt, short and shitty!")

As the man recognized his native tongue, his face greyed and he backed away from the counter, disappearing through a door at the far corner of the store. A few moments later, a young Bolivian salesclerk walked up to my father and offered his assistance. After trying on the trench coat, my father left the store with the double-breasted leather flaps unfastened. He heard them slap his chest as he walked toward his gate, dragging his alligator-skin bag.

············

The leather jacket still hangs in my parents' coat closet, darkly militaristic among the grey pea coats and bright nylon windbreakers. Because of my father's diligence in saddle-soaping his leather possessions, the trench coat seems to have broken free from time—it's as supple and saturated with shades of maroon as it was the day my father flew with it back to Canada. The jacket has hung in the closet since before I was born.

············

My father has two theories about why his switching from Spanish to German terrified the immigrant salesclerk in El Alto:

A. The man, given his age and location, was a Nazi in hiding.
B. The man, given his horror at the language, was a Holocaust survivor.

In either scenario, language morphs into a force of terror, an aphorism slips into a death threat, and instead of handwritten notes about rural water systems my father's briefcase totes a MAC-10. In either scenario, a stranger flees in mortal fear through an exit.

. . . .

In seventh grade, I began a yearlong conversation with a stranger. I never saw him in person or learned his name. Our correspondence took place daily, in pencil, scrawled across the surface of a school desk twice as old as we were: one of those hip-bone–shaped maple projectiles attached to a blue plastic chair, as if the piece were once a sleek Space Age invention—its curves and surfaces grown slowly derelict, now gouged with penknives and ossified in liver-colored gum. I began the correspondence unwittingly one day in health class by writing "I ♥ Matt" in the upper right-hand corner of my desk. The next time I sat down in my assigned seat, I noticed beneath my graffiti the words: "Matt who?"

. . . .

In the classic anthropological text *The Stranger* (1908), German sociologist Georg Simmel articulates his concept of a unique sociological form. A "peculiar tension" arises, Simmel suggests, from "the stranger," who manages to be both close to and remote from us at once. The value of such figures in society, then, stems from the stranger's "objectivity." Because they aren't intimately connected with our lives, we feel freer to confess to them our secrets. In premodern societies, Simmel writes, most strangers within a group made their living as traders, those "'strange' merchants" who move closely among us in a crowd, performing necessary tasks, even as they remain enigmatic.

. . . .

Though I have only language as proof, I like to imagine my first ancestor—the first person who claimed my surname—as a strange merchant, a traveling journeyman, dragging his carpenter's bags from village to village. The surname "Journey" comes from the French *journée,* which denotes the time span of one day. A journeyman, then, has the right to charge a fee for each day's work. Because such trades-men have completed apprenticeships but aren't yet master craftsmen who own shops, journeymen aren't fixed to one place. They may uproot and travel to other towns, improving their skills at other work-shops. The whereabouts of a journeyman can be a productive flux.

. . . .

When my father encountered his strange merchant in the leather goods shop, he felt free to forge an inside joke with the man. He felt free to belly laugh and drum his fingertips on the counter at the aphorism's off-color punch line. After all, they'd both traveled a long way to get to Bolivia. Weren't they both outsiders, facing one another across a similar distance? And yet didn't they share a closeness, too, through knowing the German tongue?

. . . .

Throughout his only book *Letters to a Stranger,* Thomas James addresses in his poems a mysterious "you." The "Thou," as Lucie Brock-Broido says in the collection's introduction, "is you; it is I; it is the beloved, the Master; it is God; he is strange, and stranger too." In the final three stanzas of the poem "Letters to a Mute," James writes to one who remains forever unable to answer:

> If I could stick my pen into your tongue,
> Making it run with gold, making
> It speak entirely to me, letting the truth

Slide out of it, I could not be alone.
I wouldn't even touch you, for I know
How you are locked away from me forever.

Tonight I go out looking for you everywhere
As the moon slips out, a slender petal
Offering all its gold to me for nothing.

There's a carnal charge to James's conditional sentence that begins, "If I could stick my pen into your tongue / Making it run with gold, making / It speak entirely to me," as if the act of giving language to the mute "you" is a wordsmith's alchemy—a Midas touch tinged with eros, rarefied and lingual. The line breaks rupture the syntax, over and over again, as the sentence extends across four lines, spilling into the next stanza before the if-clause ends in longing. If the silent one finally speaks, James suggests: "I could not be alone." Even though the poem's speaker knows such a union with the mute isn't possible, he keeps searching for the lost "you." He eschews the easy illumination of the indiscriminant moon, who'd offer "all its gold to me for nothing."

. . . .

"Matt who?" asked the stranger from another class period on the grainy surface of my seventh-grade desk. "None of your damn business," I wrote back, provoking a string of retorts: "Matt sucks"; "Matt has seven nipples"; "Matt sticks hamsters up his butt." The exchange soon lost its ire, however, probably because both graffiti scrawlers got bored staring at diagrams of genital sores or educational videos in which the grown-up actress who played Annie in the late-seventies Broadway musical talked about puberty. We switched to sharing our favorite anti-authority symbols, such as the anarchist's jagged "A" within a circle, and complaining about the high school's cold overflow trailers. We wrote "Ha!" in response to each other's wisecracks and offered advice about the best places to take narc-free smoke breaks. We wrote supportive notes like, "I know what you mean," and, "Hang in there, dude." We drew smiley faces and doodles of teachers with farting butts. The stranger and I—we needed each other.

One day, I arrived to my health class's trailer to find that Mr. Gainer had switched our assigned seats. I now sat several rows away and a couple of places up from my old desk. I gazed through the trailer's interior, the slim space jigsawed with at least thirty desks, thinking, "How are we ever going to find each other?"

. . . .

The Israeli spy agency Mossad found one of the most ruthless Nazi architects of the Holocaust, Adolf Eichmann, hiding out in Argentina, in 1960. He'd fled Germany after World War II, finally winding up in Argentina in the early fifties. Eichmann lived in the Buenos Aires area for ten years, where he assumed a false name, and worked variously as a foreman at a Mercedes-Benz factory, a junior water engineer, and a rabbit farmer. Similarly, the Gestapo captain Klaus Barbie—the "Butcher of Lyon"—fled to Argentina after working briefly for the CIA, eventually settling into a bungalow in Bolivia, which overlooked the Yungas Road. Before Barbie was extradited to France, in 1983, did he stand behind a counter at El Alto selling leather trench coats to travelers? Did he imagine the airport a house of endless escape routes? Was he comforted by the many doors? Was he soothed by the constant roar of departing planes?

. . . .

In 1975 my mother and father moved to Peine, in the German state of Lower Saxony, so my father could begin a research position in a plastic pipe manufacturing plant. For a year they lived just three miles from the memorial grounds of Bergen-Belsen. My mother asked my dad several times to come with her to visit the site of the former concentration camp, but he refused. Although my father remains a formidable history buff who can discuss with encyclopedic precision the finer points of World War II—battles, geographical terrain, political figures—the subject of the death camps stirs in him a crushing, unfathomable horror so extreme he can't bring himself to discuss it. (He feels a distinctive yet similarly acute sense of dread about the void of deep space.) Occasionally he deflects his horror of the concentration camps through humor, singing, for instance, the British song mocking the Nazi leadership called "Hitler Has Only Got One Ball," which assumes the campy, jingle-like cadences of the marching tune "Colonel Bogey March."

....

I've asked my father why he bought a coat from a shop he believed may have employed a Nazi in hiding. At the time, he assumed the German salesclerk had disappeared into the back room to locate a coat in the storage area, that because the man was older and slow the younger employee simply took over when he saw my father waiting. As my father walked to his gate, however, he began to think about the initial clerk's reaction to the German language spoken among the dark Bolivian coats. He began to wonder what associations lay beneath the language.

....

"Only in the mother tongue can one speak one's own truth," says Paul Celan.

A Holocaust survivor and French citizen of Jewish-Bukovinan descent, Celan continued to write poems in German all his life, because the language of the Gestapo who murdered his parents in the death camps was also his own native tongue. German poetry, though, as Celan understood it, needed to break free from the euphonic language of the lyre. The diction of the German lyric poem needed to become flatter, greyer, more factual, in order to contain the "sinister events in its memory." "It does not trans-figure or render 'poetical,'" Celan suggests in his *Collected Prose* (translated by Rosmarie Waldrop); "it names, it posits, it tries to measure the area of the given and the possible." In his poem "Alchemical," Celan writes (in Pierre Joris's translation from *Paul Celan: Selections*):

> Silence, cooked like gold, in
> carbonized
> hands.

> Great, gray,
> close, like all that's lost,
> sister figure:

> All the Names, all the al-
> names.

Similarly to Thomas James's "Letter to a Mute," Celan's voice-less "al- / names" remain unreachable in their silence, although the "alchemy" evoked here is utterly sinister—people are "cooked like gold" and left "carbonized." Paradoxically, what's lost remains "close"—a phantom kinship—through a dark memory, through the poem's stark echo of "All the Names."

Celan's relationship with his mother tongue remained an uneasy one. As he moved away from the lush music and surrealistic imagery of his poem "Death Fugue" and into the sparer diction and clipped syntax of "Stretto," his use of neologisms ("venomstilled," "wordblood," "heavencrazed") also increased. And although neologisms abound in German, Celan's linguistic combinations are subversively mispaired—a paradoxical uniting and sundering of sense. His strange coinages assault the German language even as they forge an unexpected intimacy—two words colliding to make an unstable, charged new sign.

From what truth did the coat salesman hide in his refusal to reply? Which sinister events—and how many names—might his speaking in German have mapped and measured?

. . . .

The speaker in Thomas James's poem "Letters to a Stranger," seated inside a church, confides:

> …the wine rides through my breast
> Like a dark hearse.
> All the while I am thinking of you.
> An avalanche of white carnations
> Is drifting across your voice
> As it drifts across the voices of confession.
> But the snow keeps whispering of you over and over.

James's speaker takes Holy Communion as if to make his absent stranger transubstantiate, but only a snow of funerary white flowers moves to reply.

. . . .

I decided to continue my "letters to a stranger" by finding my seventh-grade graffiti pen pal somewhere in the slew of reassigned seats. I returned to the former desk we shared and wrote the coordinates of my new seat. I drew a little map with a treasure chest's "X." A few days passed, and I suspected the stranger hadn't thought to check the site of our old correspondence. Then, after a week, that familiar writing drifted, once again, across the maple's waiting grain.

. . . .

I once had to write my own last name a hundred times in a row after misspelling the noun "journey" on a third-grade spelling test. I'd spelled my name correctly in the upper right-hand corner of the test, in the blank space after "Name," but I grew so anxious about screwing up on the test that, in my nervous energy, I inverted the "e" and the "n."

I like to think that my ancestor William Journey changed the spelling of his last name by deleting "man" from "Journeyman," in the late 1600s, as he departed England on a ship bound for the New World. I like to imagine he reinvented himself in the middle of the Atlantic, as he leaned against a salt-worn railing on the top deck, dreaming of tobacco fields, an unnamed creek, watching the open water foam.

. . . .

My father, William ("Tim") Journey, once hopped into the Volkswagen of a stranger in Berlin, throwing his rucksack in the backseat. It was 1964 and he was headed toward Split, Croatia, a beach town on the Dalmatian Coast, to meet two of his friends from the Free

University of Berlin. On the side of the street, he'd held up a sign on which he'd scrawled "Nuremberg," since he needed a ride that would carry him from Berlin straight through Eastern Germany, an area where hitchhiking was illegal. A young woman pulled over and offered him a lift.

During the two-hour drive, my father noticed the woman kept peering sideways at him, grinning slyly. "You recognize me, don't you?" she finally asked. My father doesn't recall his answer, though he remembers not wanting to offend the woman. He scrutinized her Bardot-like blond bouffant and black cat-eye liner. He probably nodded. She leaned over, reached into the glove box, and popped open the compartment to reveal a stack of autographed studio portraits, handing one of them to my father.

"So who was she?" I asked. He couldn't remember. "Some obscure German movie star." "What did you do with the photo?" He'd tossed it into the first trashcan he passed in Nuremberg, then thumbed for another ride. "I can't believe you threw it away!" I cried. "Weren't you curious?" My father shrugged, saying he found the movie star boring and self-absorbed. She didn't tell a single good story. "Unlike your mother," he said.

. . . .

The trench coat still hangs in my parents' downstairs closet, brought out each crisp Virginia winter by my father as he slants the tweed brim of his Greek fisherman's cap into the wind. And since before I was born, the supple sleeves of the trench must've been touched by thousands of people. By now, its dark leather's been brushed by all of us: by the countless elbows of travelers swirling through the airport store, by the palms of the Bolivian clerk who rang up my father, and by the stranger from Germany who, far from home, once crouched in the display window, lifting the heavy leather flaps over the sloped and armless torso of a plaster mannequin. As he returned to the cash register, he leaned back. He watched a man pause in front of the jacket and absently rub his shoulders as if to keep off a chill, although it was warm in Bolivia. He watched the man approach him, pointing, just beginning to open his mouth.

LITTLE FACE

"You're going to smell something," Robin said. She raised the dermatological zapper, shaped like an electric toothbrush, above the cluster of chicken pox scars pebbling my chin. "I like to call it *Korean barbecue*." The head of the fractional resurfacing device had a flat, rectangular grid at its tip that resembled a small socket—a geometric hive of evenly spaced dots. I exhaled and shut my eyes. The scent of my frying skin—so close to my own nostrils—hovered somewhere between pork meatball and snuffed match. I'd coveted other people's smooth, scar-free faces since I was thirteen. No chin-pits the width of pencil erasers. No bumpy, honeycombed cheeks. No nicknames hissed in gym class: *Hey, Swiss Cheese!* My younger sister and I spent most of our early childhoods overseas in the 1980s—five years in Bangladesh and two in India—where we faced an array of exotic calamities: my idiopathic weeklong fever that befuddled our Belgian doctor and caused me to hallucinate a flock of yawping red crows; Rebecca's encounter with a rabid dog;

my vomit-inducing head injury after I raced down the concrete steps of the American Club's restaurant, stumbled backward, and smacked my skull, concussing myself. But my sister and I never managed to catch the chicken pox as little kids. We came down with the virus a few years after moving to the United States—both of us at the same time. I was thirteen. She was ten. Soon afterward, I babysat a neighbor's three children, and one of them asked: "Why do you have holes in your skin?"

. . . .

At Oak Creek Elementary—the school where my mother works as a teacher's aide—the first-grade students annually celebrate the one hundredth day of the school year. In the past, they've honored the occasion by responding to prompts such as, "If I had one hundred dollars I would buy . . ." or, "If I could have one hundred of anything, it would be . . ." For the most recent "100th Day" celebration, however, Mrs. Hill, a first-grade teacher my mother assists, wanted to do something unusual. She gathered her students on the blue rug at one side of the classroom and wrote the following prompt on the board: "When I'm one hundred years old, I will . . ." The students raised their hands to offer suggestions: "walk with a cane," "play checkers with my grandchildren," "need a wheelchair," "have white hair," "wear a hearing aid," "be bald," "play video games all day." The six-year-olds then went back to their seats to divine a paragraph of their future biographies, beginning with the topic sentence: "When I'm one hundred years old, I will be very different."

Mrs. Hill had recently discovered an application on her iPhone that digitally aged photographs, like those time-progression programs used by police to make posters for children who've been missing for a decade. She lined up her twenty-five students in front of a wall outside of the classroom, snapped their photographs one by one with her cell phone, and digitally aged each six-year-old's chubby face and firm neck into the fuzzy upper lips and rippled jowls of a hundred-year-old. Although my mother was off assisting another class when Mrs. Hill's students first encountered the life-sized printouts, she returned later that day to help the students paste the images onto sheets of manila paper. They attached their aged faces and necks to flat, semicircular busts cut from scraps of striped or polka-dotted wallpaper.

My mother noticed that most of the students seemed dismayed or bewildered by the approximations of their future ancient selves. She watched them quietly paste and smooth their wrinkled countenances onto the paper, just above the paragraph-long "stories" of their elderly lives. Their pruned earlobes dangled like putty pressed between thumbs. Their neck folds pooled like crepe iguana wattles. Most of the boys were bald. She heard one of them say, warily, "My grandpa looks like that." Many of the centurions still sported comical, little-kid hairdos: wild silver cowlicks or white ponytails top-heavy with pink bows. Their expressions, too, remained childlike—those huge jack-o'-lantern grins—though the missing front teeth and exposed gums worked at both ends of the age spectrum. Mrs. Hill hung the twenty-five portraits in the hallway, the sagging faces arranged like a jaunty pictorial roll call decorating the lobby of a retirement community.

"These are flat disturbing," my mother said of the images to another first-grade teacher, who nodded. One especially bright child, Leo, had been so upset by his hundred-year-old face that his mother asked Mrs. Hill to remove his picture from the wall. "They're six years old," my mother told me over the phone. "They shouldn't have to internalize their own decrepitude."

. . . .

I first saw a photograph of Dr. Fredric Brandt, the world-renowned cosmetic dermatologist, a year before he hanged himself in the garage of his Coconut Grove estate in the early hours of Easter Sunday, 2015. The previous March the *New York Times* had run a largely flattering profile of Brandt, by Guy Trebay, on the front page of the "Style" section: "The Man Behind the Face." The details make Brandt sound glamorous and self-possessed: he's a sophisticated art collector who hosts his own radio show; he lives in Manhattan and Miami; he runs a company that sells his antiaging products; he's the "magician" responsible for many a celebrity's ageless face (Madonna's, John Travolta's, Naomi Campbell's). "[A] Brandt creation," Trebay writes, is "a person whose skin is smooth and yet not freakishly taut, whose cheeks possess the firm curvature of a wheel of Edam, whose unblemished flesh calls to mind a Jumeau bisque doll, a baby's bottom, or, perhaps, Madonna." Brandt's handiwork on his own plumped-up skin is, however, immediately and viscerally shocking. Due to abundant injections of botulinum toxin (Botox) and various volumizing facial fillers (Restylane, Perlane, Juvéderm, Voluma), his mid-sixties visage conjures the uncanny: it's at once ancient and infantile, foreign and familiar, a poreless rubber mask that's neither old nor young. With his wispy, Warhol-ish flaxen bob, wide ivory face, and pale grey eyes, Brandt resembles a foppish albino. His lips stretch, broad and froglike, puffed up and tea-rose pink. All bags and lines have been wiped from beneath his eyes. In one photograph, Brandt resembles a Scandinavian vampire posed in black leather pants, a jet velvet blazer, and designer high-tops in front of an Albert Oehlen painting. (The artwork's focal point features the face of an androgynous blond in which a dark flesh-colored "X" blots out the nose and most of the figure's expression.) In another photograph, Brandt emotes with a strange, open-mouthed pucker at a party for Lady

Gaga's fragrance launch at the Guggenheim, a black Colombina carnival mask dangling by the elastic around his neck. As I glanced at Brandt's image for the first time, I gasped, shaking the paper wordlessly in front of my husband's face.

. . . .

The word *face* derives from the Latin *facies* (form, appearance) and, according to the *Oxford English Dictionary*, it crops up in a number of expressions:

> To *fly in the face of,* meaning "to do the opposite of," is recorded from the 16th century. It is taken literally from the notion of a dog attacking someone by springing directly at them. To *lose face,* meaning to be humiliated, is a direct translation of a Chinese phrase. The 16th-century dramatist Christopher Marlowe coined the phrase *the face that launched a thousand ships* to describe the great beauty of Helen, whose abduction by Paris caused the Trojan War. Facet (early 17th century) is literally a "little face" from French *facette*.

Did Brandt's artificial appearance *fly in the face of* conventional cosmetic dogma, which celebrates the ways aging people might look plausibly youthful? According to Lili Anolik's article in *Vanity Fair*, Brandt projected a goofy, self-aware sense of humor about his highly stylized appearance, which he seemed to regard as a sort of costume or performance of camp. "Fred was famous for interrupting patients in the middle of a consult," Anolik writes, "saying, 'But enough about how you look. How do *I* look?,' followed by a wild shriek of laughter." In order to put squeamish clients at ease, he referred to Botox and filler by friendly-uncle-sounding nicknames: "Bo and Phil." But did he *lose face* by stilling the nerves in his own? Was his "the face that launched a thousand jokes," as online commentators mocked his *Times* profile? He read all of the posts. One person compared Brandt to "a character from a Wes Craven film." Another suggested "an 80 year old trying to look 64." Yet another wrote: "I wouldn't let that butcher cut baloney."

....

"I'd go with filler," the head dermatologist, known profession-ally as Amy MD, said after scrutinizing my chicken pox scars. I kicked my legs back and forth like a child as I perched at the edge of the elevated exam chair and imagined Dr. Brandt's alien face. An ancient baby. It reminded me of the ghoulish portraits on the wall outside of my mother's first-grade classroom. "When I think of filler," I blurted, "I think *freak show*." Amy MD peered at me over her clipboard. She was a brunette of indeterminate age who'd recently begun hosting her own cable dermatology show, which played on a hypnotic, product-hawking loop amid the lobby's maple-and-linen Zen décor. She appeared unmoved by my reac-tion. Due to my horror of injections—especially in the face, espe-cially with that Dr. Frankenstein filler (some fillers use collagen harvested from pig corpses or medical cadavers)—we agreed I'd try a heat-based treatment called "fractional resurfacing," which stimulates collagen production through targeted bursts of radio waves. "Your scars are subtle," Amy MD said, as she looked down toward her clipboard again, "but they're there."

....

Two years after chicken pox left pink dents in my face, I went through a period in ninth grade when I deliberately inflicted scars on my skin. Alone in my room, I'd run my lighter across the bottom wire of a coat hanger and press the hot steel into my left bicep, repeating the gesture until I'd made three parallel burns that puffed into long blisters. The marks eventually blanched from a row of pink worms to a white, clawlike print, as if I were a bumbling falconer who let a hawk land on her bare arm. Other times I'd sit on the concrete steps in front of my house and play the Cigarette Game with my friend Laura. We'd press our forearms together—forming a mirror image—and one of us would light a Camel, puff on the filter to get a cherry going, and drop the cigarette in the valley between our arms. The first to pull away from the burn lost the contest. Although watching the damage unfold fascinated me, it was easier to win if I stared at a nearby pine.

Laura and I lost touch toward the end of that spring, after she got pregnant unexpectedly and dropped out of high school. More than twenty years later, the nine white cigarette burns on my right arm are at once marks of healing and traces of what won't ever entirely fade away. They remind me that there's a woman out there who reaches for a dinner fork, who drives to the grocery store, who brushes a strand of black hair from her neck, all the while wearing an identical set.

. . . .

My seventh-grade science teacher, Mrs. Tart, a silver-haired woman in her mid-fifties, wore a dusty surfeit of terra-cotta rouge in unblended circles on her cheeks. The students in the class used to mock her doll-like makeup, whispering to each other across the desks. We called her Krusty the Clown, after a character on *The Simpsons*. When I finally returned to school after my two-week absence, Mrs. Tart noticed my fresh chicken pox scars and suggested to my mother at Back-to-School Night that perhaps once I got older I might have a facial peel. She must've seen the way I sat with my head tilted forward so my long hair closed over my cheeks. I don't remember why I bought a container of cheap fuchsia blush from CVS, tied it in a red ribbon, curled the bow's edges with a scissor's blade, and secretly tossed the gift on her desk on the last day of class. I'd taped an unsigned note to it: "Dear Mrs. Tart, Why don't you use some more blush!" Or maybe: "Have some more blush, Mrs. Tart!" Did someone dare me to do it? Did I brag about the prank afterward and feel like a punk-rock badass? Or did I feel ashamed? I was terribly shy in middle school. As far as I remember, I never teased other students. What combination of vulnerability and vindictiveness must've roused my capacity for cruelty, and created, like the opposing visages of the Roman god Janus, another face?

The likelihood that Mrs. Tart layered a heavy impasto of rouge across her cheeks to mask her insecurities about her own complexion didn't seem to penetrate my adolescent narcissism or deter my viciousness. Perhaps I saw in her elaborately made-up face my own recent damage, as well as my inability to conceal it. Mrs. Tart never mentioned the incident. I've often wondered if she suspected it was me who made that most unfunny joke: the quiet girl in the front row who daily slathered nude foundation—always a shade too dark—over her own pale face.

. . . .

Until Fredric Brandt's suicide, I hadn't recalled that hateful seventh-grade prank for decades. I sat down with my morning latte, and in the *New York Times* was the headline: "Dr. Fredric Brandt, 65, Celebrity 'Baron of Botox,' Is Dead." Guy Trebay, the same author who'd composed the glamorous "Style" profile on the doctor a year earlier, had written Brandt's grim obituary. "Susan Biegacz, a publicist for Dr. Brandt," Trebay notes, "said he had been dealing with depression for some time and had recently been 'devastated' by what is widely believed to be a parody of him on the Tina Fey comedy series *Unbreakable Kimmy Schmidt*, presented by Netflix."

The next day, flying from Los Angeles to an annual conference in Minneapolis, I obsessed about Brandt. And each of the four nights at the conference, I searched for articles about his death as I sat in my hotel room, haunted by that blank, unnerving face. In the aftermath of Brandt's suicide, some people blamed his death on the televised joke. In the episode, Martin Short plays a demented dermatologist whose overuse of Botox has caused a freakish speech impediment in which the doctor is no longer able to pronounce his own name, which is Dr. Grant. Short sputters a slobbery approximation—"Dr. Franff"—as he leaks drool from his greasy, rubberized face and leaps around the office in a white lab coat like a mad scientist. As Anolik writes in *Vanity Fair*: "That the doctor with the peroxided bob and face of a dissipated cherub, the skin as slick and shiny as a glazed doughnut whom Jacqueline Voorhees (Jane Krakowski) visits for a foot facelift, is intended to be Fred is beyond question." Two weeks before he killed himself, Brandt sent his coworker—Anolik's husband—a text message after reading about the unflattering caricature in the gossip column "Page Six": "Did u see page 6 I'm so upset I'm a freak." However unfunny Anolik found Short's performance on *Kimmy Schmidt*, she refuses to blame Brandt's suicidal despair on satire. "For what it's worth," she writes, "I think the idea is loony. If the show did, in fact, push him over the edge, that could only be because he had one foot and four toes curled over it already."

I had watched the now-infamous episode of *Unbreakable Kimmy Schmidt* with my husband several weeks before Brandt's death. Although we'd both read the *Times* profile on the dermatologist a year earlier, neither of us managed to recognize Brandt in the caricature—we'd forgotten about him—and neither of us laughed. The gag seemed too obvious, like bad *Saturday Night Live* slapstick: the cosmetic dermatologist who turned himself into a monster. Brandt was already a joke: the doctor who could no longer recall the biblical proverb, "Physician, heal thyself."

. . . .

In the fairy tale "The Old Man Made Young Again," recounted in the early nineteenth century by Jacob and Wilhelm Grimm, Jesus and St. Peter stop at a blacksmith's house one evening for food and lodging. Later that night, a disfigured old man arrives at the same house, ill and begging for alms. St. Peter pities the elder and asks Jesus to perform a miracle so that the beggar might be restored to youth and able to earn money to buy his own bread. Jesus asks the blacksmith for help:

> "Smith, lend Me thy forge, and put on some coals for Me, and then I will make this ailing old man young again." The smith was quite willing, and St. Peter blew the bellows, and when the coal fire sparkled up large and high our Lord took the little old man, pushed him into the forge in the midst of the red-hot fire, so that he glowed like a rose bush, and praised God with a loud voice. After the Lord went to the quenching tub, put the glowing little man into it so that the water closed over him, and after He had carefully cooled him, gave him His blessing, when behold! the little man sprang nimbly out, looking fresh, straight, healthy, and as if he were but twenty.

The blacksmith, impressed by the beggar's miraculous transformation, decides to make his crooked old mother-in-law young
again. After all, it was his own blacksmith's forge and bellow that
the Lord had used to work the miracle, and who was in a better
position to wield those tools than an expert? The next day, Jesus
and St. Peter depart, unaware of the blacksmith's plan. The latter
asks his aged mother-in-law if she'd like to be turned into a girl
of eighteen. "'With all my heart,'" she answers, "'as the youth has
come out so well.'" "So the smith made a great fire," the Brothers
Grimm write:

> and thrust the old woman into it, and she writhed
> about this way and that, and uttered terrible cries of
> murder. "Sit still; why art thou screaming and jump-
> ing about so?" cried he, and as he spoke he blew the
> bellows again until all her rags were burnt. The old
> woman cried without ceasing, and the smith thought
> to himself, "I have not quite the right art," and took
> her out and threw her into the cooling tub. Then
> she screamed so loudly that the smith's wife upstairs
> and her daughter-in-law heard, and they both ran
> downstairs, and saw the old woman lying in a heap
> in the quenching-tub, howling and screaming, with
> her face wrinkled and shriveled and all out of shape.

. . . .

A face has over forty muscles, nearly seven thousand unique expressions. As social creatures, we fixate on faces, seek out cues and clues,
read their fine lines. There's a reason small children draw—almost
exclusively—faces. Have you ever remembered someone by the fine
shape of her right foot? Tenderly recalled a great-uncle's distinctive

elbow? Have you ever glimpsed in a patterned surface—in a spot of fleur-de-lis wallpaper or the mottled calcium of an oyster shell or the knobby burl of a redwood—the uncanny textures of a face? Brandt erased what made his face human. He muted all nuance, collapsing many facets into one: a deadpan, bovine impassivity. It's easy to loathe a frozen face. It hides its experiences, suffering, and delights—the signals the shy twitch of a lip sends out, a smile that creases the eye. It obliterates that deep nonverbal richness of gesture. That's why I reflexively despised Brandt before I learned that he was a funny, sad, and fragile man—why I gasped the first time I saw his photograph. I didn't know he lived alone in his Coconut Grove mansion with three adopted dogs: Tyler, Surya, and Benji. I didn't know he was fifteen when his diabetic father died, twenty when he lost his mother. I didn't know his radio show got canceled. I didn't know Brandt longed to "restore a face to harmony," as if wiping away the world's wrinkles could blot out the losses in his life. His blank face gave away none of his empathy or anguish; it made him alien, other, the freak against which we define ourselves.

. . . .

The fractional resurfacing device didn't erase all of the chicken pox scars on my face. It did, however, cause collagen to plump up the shallow ones: two on my left cheek, three on my chin, one on my nose, two on my forehead. The deep triple pit gouging my upper right cheek is still there—the one in which a trio united to form a single trench, the one I used to fantasize about spackling with peanut butter or even concrete—but it's softer, no longer immediately noticeable as a crater. A stranger would probably need to squint at close-up before and after pictures to discern any difference. But I know what it's like to stand an inch from the bathroom mirror and scrutinize every mark and scar. I understand something of what Brandt must've wanted to hide by revising his skin. I'm reminded, each time I think of Brandt's death, of my phone call to a suicide hotline during a breakdown years earlier, and I know his choice shocks me so acutely because it could've been my own. When I look at Brandt, I recognize something like an alter ego, the vulnerable side of myself I'd rather not see—its self-loathing, its impulsiveness, its vanity. I imagine the Roman god Janus who stands in doorways and wears two faces, one on the front and one of the back of his head—maybe they're mine and Brandt's—one facet fixed on an exit and the other, tipped toward an entrance, hoping—no, deciding—to venture on.

A FLICKER OF ANIMAL, A FLANK

There's a difference between leaving and abandoning a place. As in: I left Richmond, Virginia, once. After eight years, I was ready to leave for Texas. As in: then I moved back and abandoned it. Both kinds of departure may seem, from the outside (to a neighbor who doesn't know your name, a server in the corner café), indistinguishable. Leaving is easy. You throw a bouquet of spatulas and wooden spoons in the extra two inches of room in a box packed with novels. You tape the seam shut. You mark the calendar. You circle the exact date. There's a more nuanced art to navigating the layers of abandonment. To renounce, reject, disown, desert, forsake, or to quit a place, it has to have wounded you the way a person can.

Maybe I prefer the word *quit* to *abandon*. I like the verb's tragicomic, cowgirlish edge, its sassy monosyllable. As in: moving to a one-bedroom apartment in a lavender Victorian on the grounds of an old riverside cemetery just after a breakup was a bad idea. I quit the bay windows and floor-length red drapes. I quit the wraparound porch. I quit the antique rocker I thought I saw bob by itself next to my bed at night. I quit the weekday whirr of the groundskeeper's lawnmower buzzing *the beautiful uncut hair of graves.*

. . . .

According to the *Oxford English Dictionary*, "abandon" derives from the Old French *abandoner*. The word comes from the Latin *ad* ("to, at") and *bannus* ("control"). The verb's original sense meant the exact opposite of its current definition. Abandon used to mean to "bring under control." Later, it became "give in to the control of, surrender to."

. . . .

I surrender eight years, four apartments, two college degrees, a tree-thronged street named Cherry, my old potter's smock, one brick row house painted eggshell blue, one lone white crepe myrtle in the backyard and its faux snow. I surrender one slow opaque Virginia river named for an English king, James. I surrender the yellow-painted head shop on Grace and its spiced wall of clove cigarettes, fragrant in their black papers. I surrender my usual order: veggie sausage, egg, and cheddar on a kaiser. I surrender, like Robert E. Lee, whose bronze statue is rooted in the grass roundabout on Monument Avenue, the cars moving in circles at his conquered feet. In winter, the weak sunlight shines on the general's southward-tipped face instead of the creased ass cheeks of his horse, Traveller. Why did we ever stop calling people *horse's ass?* As in: I was a real horse's ass to cheat on my former boyfriend, who was a good man. As in: my friend was a horse's ass for ratting me out. For judging me, doubling my losses. When did *abandon* pivot, like a cast figure come to life or an old friend, furious, turning to face that exact opposite direction?

. . . .

The abandoned zoo, called "The Old Zoo," in Los Angeles's Griffith Park, is a ghost town: quiet, acute, hypnotic with graffiti. It was built in 1912 and closed in 1966, the animals shipped off, relocated. I visit the site with my husband. A sandy, briar-edged trail winds through a labyrinth of vacant animal grottos, man-made caves, and empty iron cages with their ochre-tinged doors hanging open. Almost every structure's swaddled in chain link, the fences torqued and perforated with wire cutters to create thorny birch-leaf–shaped doors. A repeated graffiti tag says *PAST*, in sweeping all-capital letters: blue over stone, red over desert cliff, red over dented-tin wall of a metal house (of reptiles? small mammals?). I pose for a photograph, crouched inside a person-sized birdcage, and poke my fingers through the spindly crosshatched wires. I snap some shots from within a square enclosure (for wildcats? gorillas?), its wrist-thick iron bars blotting long strips from the weeping silver-dollar eucalyptus. In my peripheral vision, I keep thinking I see a flicker of animal, a flank. I take a whole series of close-ups of lumpy, archaic keyholes, the rusted-hazel spaces of the cages behind them empty except for the ancient ivy's helix threatening to break through. On a hill, we watch a professional photographer pace the sepia stubble in front of his subject and see the ivory pleats of a black-haired girl's airy quinceañera dress weave alternating tiers of shadow and light.

. . . .

The tattoo artist who gave me a tour of his apartment on the grounds of the graveyard in Richmond, which I rented for a month and then abandoned, called himself Captain Morgan, like the Jamaican rum named for the Welsh pirate. He had spiky blond hair and dense sleeves of greenish ink covering his shoulders, forearms, hands, knuckles, and neck. Captain Morgan was about to leave his one-bedroom on the first floor of the former groundskeeper's house to move farther south and open a new tattoo boutique. At the time, I felt like a captain, too: that grizzled seafarer from Coleridge's *The Rime of the Ancient Mariner* cursed with the compulsion to repeat his story of a haunted voyage over and over again, to anyone who would listen. Captain Morgan listened to me, though, with empathy and patience. Over brunch and mimosas that simmered in our noses as we sipped, he told me a few anecdotes of his own. He'd recently reunited with an old girlfriend from art school and planned to follow her to Nashville. He recalled several of the most memorable designs he'd given people (a hand tattoo of a woman biting a ball gag, a half-sleeve depicting the Wicked Witch of the West, a small wing behind the ear of a Croatian occultist). He also told me about the time he visited the two-room shack in Tupelo where Elvis was born.

Before we parted, Captain Morgan led me to a burled fiddleback armoire stationed in the bedroom that he said came with the apartment, since the piece was solid walnut and much too heavy to move. It had been left behind by a previous tenant, and by the one before that. Captain Morgan opened the armoire's French doors and raised what looked like the bottom plank of the interior closet to reveal a secret storage compartment lined with plum-colored velvet. Weeks later, after I'd moved in, I peeked into the armoire's hidden chamber to find a present Captain Morgan had stashed there for me: a large hardcover art book I'd admired on his coffee table, a collection of Alberto Vargas's vintage illustrations of pinups, voluptuous and leggy and often nude except for a pair of black sling-backs or a shouldered mink stole. As a tattoo artist, Captain Morgan had etched a number of naked Vargas-like ladies onto the rippling biceps of men (and women, too, he said), who'd flex and bring the twitching figures to life. My two favorite Vargas illustrations date from the early 1920s and feature ethereally pale, dark-haired women with jagged flapper bobs poised in fantastic settings. In *Dragonfly* (1922), a nude woman turns her sleek, marbled back to the viewer, two transparent, eye-spotted insect wings socketed to her shoulder blades. As she leans to sniff a white rose, her hefty cone-shaped left breast dips its nipple into a lower blossom. In *Nita Naldi* (1923), the silent film actress—naked except for a gold rope choker, dangling earrings, snake bracelet, and oval obsidian ring—drapes her elegant arms around a marble bust of Pan. Naldi's bold, kohl-lined gaze catches the viewer's directly, while the goat-horned god grins impishly into her temple. Her warm flesh tones brighten next to the sculpture's cold stone. As I flipped through the pages, the women seemed to pulse and multiply in my silent apartment, stretched on chaise lounges or peering over bare shoulders or clutching ruffled parasols with slender fingers, their tips polished red.

. . . .

Vargas drew the two nude flappers during the time the Old Zoo bustled with visitors wearing similar Jazz Age haircuts, when the place was musky with the scent of oily bears and the fermented tang of sweet hay matted in the dung of elephants. More than ninety years later I mistake the muggy, urinous scent for the funk of animals, but instantly realize the unlikeliness that the original odor could have lingered for so long. Teenagers must've gotten drunk and peed on the graffitied walls and mossy corners. But I'd read in the *New Yorker* about a treasure-hunting diver who found the ruins of a pirate ship at the bottom of the sea. He disturbed a layer of silt above the wreck and recognized the unmistakable stench of piss, the scent by then three centuries old.

When I look at the book Captain Morgan placed in the antique armoire I remember a kindness I deeply needed, a camaraderie offered by a stranger who'd taken a pirate's name. I knew Captain Morgan for maybe an hour, yet his gifts to me have meant everything: his patience, his stories, his sly offering waiting within our shared space. I left Richmond once, I abandoned it once, and when I return to it now, I return as a visitor. Sometimes it feels like a ruin and other times I brush up against the layered populations and faint aromas of ghosts: my old selves, former friends, vanished lovers. They wander the wisteria-flaked alleys, scattered with lavender, as the cracks in the brick below give way to another century's cobblestones. Then surrender to another's. Sometimes the cracks feel that deep, that close.

PANGAEA FOR ALICE

The wisteria vine that winds up my deck's trellis spirals clockwise in California, advancing its thick, linear timeline. It knots with my nostalgia each time I think of my old life on the opposite coast. Its motion reminds me I can't go back to Richmond, Virginia.

Weak and not self-supporting, Virginia wisteria climbs iron fences, wooden trellises, telephone poles, cable wires, nineteenth-century gravestones, lampposts, balconies, carriage houses, roofs, and garages in a counterclockwise swirl, hurling itself backward—against time—toward the city's older core. The vines twist through Richmond's cobblestone alleys mosaicked in grey ovals—those smooth, turkey-egg–shaped stones paved before the Civil War. They drape the green, Victorian grounds of Maymont—Major James H. Dooley's Gilded Age estate—thatching a lavender ceiling for the Italian Garden's marble pergola and spiraling its ivory columns. They stipple their violet impasto behind the legend of Edgar rumored to ghost the street near Poe's Pub on East Main, his

broad forehead creased as if considering the tangle of slow vines—
Monet's night terror.

. . . .

Flamboyant as a drag queen's wig, wild as a psychedelic grapevine,
wisteria was named by the botanist Thomas Nuttall after Caspar
Wistar, an eighteenth-century white-haired Quaker. Wistar—a
Philadelphia physician, paleontologist, and professor of anatomy—
taught for over thirty years at the University of Pennsylvania. A
popular academic, Wistar enlivened his lectures with colorful
teaching aids, some of which included ghoulish anatomical models
comprised of actual human organs and limbs, which he'd dried and
injected with wax. Outside of the classroom, Wistar hosted weekly
salons for local and visiting intellectuals known as "Wistar parties"
in which guests, such as the French botanist François Andre Mich-
aux and the Portuguese diplomat and naturalist, the Abbé Cor-
rêa da Serra, discussed politics, art, science, and philosophy. "The
company met," recalled the physician Charles Caldwell, "without
ceremony, on a stated evening, where in the midst of a succession
of suitable refreshments, the time passed away, oftentimes until a
late hour, in agreeable, varied, and instructive discourse." Wistar
also founded the Society for Circulating the Benefit of Vaccination.
He belonged to the Humane Society, the Pennsylvania Prison Society, the Literary and Philosophical Society of New York, and the
Society for the Abolition of Slavery, the latter of which he become
president in 1813. In 1791 Wistar had bought and freed a slave "to
extricate him from that degraded Situation."

. . . .

Richmond braids in its fraught layers the degradation of Man-
chester Docks, that former port in the downriver slave trade, as

well as the eclectic hum of Virginia Commonwealth University, the diverse arts-centered school that unites the old pawn shops and new foodie restaurants of downtown with the genteel bay windows and crepe myrtled courtyards of the Fan District, the narrow row houses and mossy cemetery of Oregon Hill, and the drywall-shuttered windows and torn chain link of Jackson Ward. I went to art school as an undergraduate at VCU, stooped over a pottery wheel most nights in the ceramics studio on Broad Street as I mouthed the words to Grateful Dead songs blasting from the Discman in my smock's front pocket. Each time I rose from the wheel to rinse my clay-covered arms in the industrial sink, wider than two side-by-side bathtubs, I passed my reflection in the panoramic black windows of the studio, my torso lit and climbing with the city's lights. After my art degree, I earned my MFA in creative writing at VCU; and all through those eight years in the city, I'd take shortcuts to campus, winding my way through the cobblestone alleys.

The word "shortcut," though, may be misleading. An alley in Richmond won't let you scramble to get to class. Try and rush and you'll twist your ankle in the gaping pit of a missing cobblestone or stub a couple of vertebrae as you stomp on the dome of an irregular pebble and compress the bones of your lower spine. I chose the erratic routes for their baroque tangles of foliage: those dazzling violet hedges of wisteria that warped—big as willows—over brick walls, snowing their flakes of lavender between the cobbles' cracks. For the way the alleys slowed everything down.

. . . .

Only an aging greyhound slows down. The gaunt beasts that race around the dog tracks near Houston can reach over forty miles per hour. The animals sprint counterclockwise on the circular track, chasing a mechanical decoy rabbit that zips ahead of them on a raised parallel rail, powered by an electric motor. I've tried at least three times to write a poem in which the figure of Lewis Carroll's Alice slips from the bleachers at a Texas greyhound racing track, enchanted by the whirring speed of the plastic white rabbit. As she stands in the center of the arena, the stampeding dogs swirl around her. Their rapid counterclockwise movements kick up a dry, umber dust, spiraling her back into the past. In my version of Wonderland, Alice morphs into a trippy, cowgirlish time traveler among the fried gulf shrimp and drunken cheers and skeletal dogs, their brindled fur blurring to one smooth shade of red. Each time I try to write this poem, Alice slips deeper into the center of the teeming track, back into the past, without me.

. . . .

As far as I know, wisteria won't grow in Houston, a place hostile to many species of plants as well as types of people. The shrub's rumored to spring up in the moist forests near the wide state's eastern swamps, though I've never seen the evidence. I lived in Houston for three and a half years while earning my doctorate, dragging my then-boyfriend, Carrick, from Virginia with me. We used to hike the Texas trails beside the sulfurous white oak swamps and algaed bayous, eager to see flashes of will-o'-the-wisp through the trees, sparked from the water's occasional lisps of methane. Instead we once startled a herd of javelina gathered at the edge of a shallow finger lake at twilight and ducked, squealing, behind the trunk of a live oak as the bristled animals charged by, snorting and tossing their hoglike snouts. Of course, Houston had its share of beguiling flora: the loose impressionistic crepe myrtles; the barbed gold tongues of hibiscus; the looming droop-necked sunflowers as tall as bookcases; the bulbous-tipped tulip trees that were all fuchsia-striped white petals—to hell with any green leaves. But I had no use for highways lit with neon crosses, for top-heavy Spanish moss, for sliced brisket that barbecued my fingerprints with its frottage of vinegar.

. . . .

The first time I met my undergraduate poetry teacher, Lee, who became my long-term mentor and one of my closest friends in Richmond, he rushed into class ten minutes late wearing a black leather jacket, brown beard, and air of subversive authority that suited a man whose telephone had been tapped by the FBI during the early 1970s for antiwar activism and whose elaborate yarn-spinning in the classroom reminded us that he'd abandoned his plan to attend the Catholic seminary to become a poet. Poetry is the supreme fiction, Lee told us, quoting Wallace Stevens. Don't cede any damn territory to fiction writers, he preached, pushing our allegiance as novice writers away from fact and toward imagination. The gospel according to Lee, we said. Amen.

Lee took seriously my beginner's poems, his meticulous comments—blue pen, all caps—filling the negative space. He pulled books from his shelves or printed copies of poems from his computer, read them aloud, and taught me how to talk and think about poetry. Two hours would slip by, as I sat, fixed to my chair, by turns laughing and annotating poems. Other times we'd pick up Carrick and hike the trails in Pocahontas State Park or drive to Sugar Hollow or cross the suspension footbridge over the James River to get to Belle Isle. Often the three of us would meet at 821 Café on Cary Street, the narrow punk-rock diner next door to an abandoned brick bakery with a graffito bust of the late poet Larry Levis spray-painted on its front door, behind a punctured wire screen that flapped in the wind like grey veil. In the portrait, Levis had thick furrowed brows, a furtive sideways glance, and a bushy mustache that resembled that of an earlier poet who once lived and wrote in Richmond: Edgar Allan Poe. During one of our first meetings, Lee taught me Levis's poem "Slow Child with a Book of Birds" in which a "slow child" on a bus shows the speaker a picture of a snowy egret in a guide book, mispronouncing the bird's name as "No Regrets." The poem veers back and forth through history, swirling together Samuel Taylor Coleridge as he witnesses two American sailors torture a pelican on board a ship; François Villon admiring the carnivorous ardor of crows pecking out the eyes of thieves lashed to a scaffold; and a woman "slipping her black tank top off without a word" at a party, who then "whispers the nonsense / of 'Wooly Bully'" in the speaker's ear. At the end of the poem, Levis zooms in with cinematic precision on the naïve child's junk food–occluded grin and then telescopes outward again:

> No regrets, some food still stuck
> Between his teeth in his off-white, foolish,
> Endless grin, that unrelenting music
> That makes all things a scattering & wheeling
> Once again, the black seeds thrown out onto
> The snow & window squealing shut just after—
> The sudden, overcast quiet of the past tense.

. . . .

In 1793, the same year the yellow fever epidemic blazed through the state, Caspar Wistar joined the staff of the Pennsylvania Hospital. While helping his close friend and colleague Benjamin Rush fight the epidemic, Wistar himself contracted the disease, became seriously ill, and nearly died. Wistar and Rush clashed over approaches to treating yellow fever, and their opposing beliefs about bleeding and purging finally ended their friendship.

. . . .

I've learned that, like friendship, wisteria climbs in one of two directions: clockwise or counterclockwise. Noticing the direction of a particular plant's spiral is one way to determine its species. The botanical term *dextrorse* denotes a leftward twinning (clockwise) wisteria while the term *sinistrorse* refers to rightward-spiraling (counterclockwise) vines. The fragrant, grape-bunch-shaped bouquet of each wisteria shoot is a fluffy structure called a raceme, and contains the thick base of the stalk—the peduncle—which thins into the wispier rachis, off of which shoot smaller stems, or pedicles, that bloom pale lilac flowers.

. . . .

In the cobblestone alley that linked South Cherry and South Laurel—my street and Lee's—behind the row house I rented with Carrick in Oregon Hill, a wisteria vine draped the top half of a wooden fence, dangling its ethereal racemes over a pair of black garbage cans. Each fall and winter, I'd almost forget about the shrub as it receded into a skeleton. Completely bare of flowers and leaves, it resembled a harvested grapevine. In spring the wisteria would flower and join the crepe myrtles in dropping lavenders, pinks, and whites over the smooth blue cobbles.

. . . .

Bayou Two O'Clock, Clara Mack, Pondside Blue. Some wisteria species sound like the names of bluegrass bands, pioneer women, or lesser-known jazz standards. Others recall bad poem titles (Amethyst Falls), facial rashes (Rosea), or German skin creams (Nivea). We've lost a number of unique shades and shapes of wisteria to extinction: the long, compact racemes of the violet Backhousiana, the deep purple tufts of Purpurea. There's even a form of Kentucky Wisteria that blooms a rare starched white.

. . . .

In addition to his ties to the delicate blossoming shrub of the pea family, wisteria's Quaker namesake was also honored in the moniker of a certain inbred strain of white rat used for medical research, the Wistar rat. Wistar rats originated in the 1930s at the Wistar Institute of Anatomy and Biology in Philadelphia, which was named after the good professor. So the father of wisteria is also the pater of the iconic red-eyed lab rat.

. . . .

Lee's first encounter with a rat occurred in 1950s Missouri, when his fiery, working-class adoptive mother discovered the vermin perched on the edge of his crib and allegedly fired at it with her pistol. I don't remember whether Lee said she hit her target or if the rat died. I do recall Lee's pride in his adoptive mother's fierce loyalty, however, which he contrasted with his birth mother's rejection. He'd joke, darkly, that he had a lump on his skull attained when he was yanked from his mother by the deforming tongs of midcentury medical forceps. He'd once tracked down his birth mother—at a girlfriend's urging—drove to Missouri and telephoned her, hoping to arrange a visit. She was by then in her eighties, a former Ozarkian wild woman, Lee said, and mother of at least eight other children. She either couldn't recall giving Lee up for adoption, due to the haze of advanced dementia, or didn't wish to acknowledge him. She hung up the phone.

. . . .

Caspar Wistar collected his medical lectures and published a two-volume treatise, *A System of Anatomy*, in 1811 and 1814. In the chapter titled "Of the Heart and the Pericardium, and the Great Vessels Connected with the Heart," Wistar writes: "The muscular fibres of the heart are generally less florid than those of the voluntary muscles: they are also more closely compacted together. The direction of many of them is oblique or spiral."

. . . .

The direction of my friendship with Lee is oblique or spiral. He finally ended our decade-long bond after he learned, from his fiancée, that I'd cheated on Carrick. Outraged, he told my ex and they both stopped speaking to me. I understood Lee's feelings of betrayal. To a degree, I even understood his actions, too: that latent Catholic in him emerging, finally, flush-faced from behind the pulpit.

When we finally reconciled, nearly two years later, our friendship felt pale, vulnerable, wary. I'd become that wisteria vine circling its point of origin, growing ever more distant from it, or that passenger on the bus in Levis's "Slow Child with a Book of Birds," seated in the ironic echo chamber of the boy who repeats the warped and reverberating name of the snowy egret: "No Regrets."

. . . .

Maybe I don't need a pack of counterclockwise-racing greyhounds to spiral Alice—and myself—back to the past. I have the time-warped alleys of Richmond, those narrow corridors of stillness through the city's rush of traffic, above kayakers whirling in the James River's ochre rapids, beside students walking to VCU. As soon as someone enters an alley, the wisteria-shrouded path stops time. The vines erase all signs of contemporaneity: they hide the shiny tops of sedans parked behind row houses, climb the silver bowls of now defunct TV satellites, canopy children's blue plastic swings that dangle from pin oaks. Without these modern markers, the wisteria-topped gates barbed with cast-iron magnolia buds might as well fence another century. Yet they form a permeable border. Why not believe Poe might mosey around the corner at any minute, his tussled hair frizzy from the Virginia humidity? Each time I walk though Richmond's winding alleys, gestural with high hedges of wisteria, I step into an ancient landscape.

. . . .

Over the telephone, my father told me that the reason Chinese wisteria and the woody shrubs that cover Appalachia look so similar is because they were once entangled in the forests of the same region: Pangaea, that ancient landmass in which all the fragments of our world existed in a single irregular plane. The probable configuration of Pangaea, mapped with contemporary geographical borders, resembles a child's wobbly drawing of a parrot: Eurasia (beak and head), North America (breast), South America (belly), Africa and Arabia (wing), India (lower back), Antarctica (leg), Australia (tail feathers). Somewhere in the "neck" portion of the three-hundred-million-year-old parrot, the original wisteria knitted together its network of lavenders, until the landmass began to break apart, about one hundred million years ago, at the start of continental drift. "It's all very wisterious," my father deadpanned.

. . . .

Like Wistar's and Rush's, my friendship with Lee had split in a sudden continental drift. I don't remember most of our last telephone conversation before the rift. "You're a deceiver," Lee had shouted. I remember hanging up on him—or did he hang up on me?—and the way that final severing seemed to echo and shake every wiry hair of the Spanish moss outside like a shivering ghost wisteria. The way it fractured me from my past that had seemed, until that point, so whole, stable, retraceable.

. . . .

In Levis's vision, the present and past swirl together, the poem itself becoming "that unrelenting music / That makes all things a scattering & wheeling / Once again . . . ." The lyric moment seems to braid both directions of the winding wisteria at once, its clockwise growth toward some future and its counterclockwise movement into the past. I often feel that I'm growing in both directions at once, that I continue to reside, stubborn outlaw, in both provinces. Or maybe this space is like a cobblestone that I've stomped on for the hundredth time, which wiggles loose so I can stoop and carry it in my palm or pocket. *No Regrets.* So, I claim for my past one extinct raceme of the violet Backhousiana, one pedicle plucked from its vanished lilac expanse. Surely I can burden a tuft of wisteria with eight years, with the streets named Grove, Hanover, Park, and Cherry. It can carry all the cobblestones, the poetry teacher, the old boyfriend, the clay-covered smock, the girl cross-legged in the graveyard with a lapful of poems, Edgar Allan Poe, Larry Levis, Caspar Wistar, his wisteria vines in the alleys twisting, with the hands of my clock, slowly back.

A COMMON SKIN

The first time I rode a horse after nearly three decades out of the saddle, the grilled asparagus I ate later that day tasted like the smell of a stable, like hay dust, leather, and sweat. While Proust had his madeleine, I had the grassy synesthesia of a scaled vegetable. For two years when I was six and seven, my family lived overseas in New Delhi, where I took English riding lessons, a mix of dressage and jumping. I've discovered that my body retains the muscle memory of that time, though none of the suppleness. I can recall the proper motions—the posting diagonals, the low heels, the "light seat"— but my ass keeps crashing down on the cantle, smacking the horse's back. I used to be able to sync my rise and fall with the two-beat rhythm of a trot, keeping my crotch tipped toward the curve of the pommel, but now my pelvis slips back and my shoulders plunge forward, my body stiff and off-kilter, one stunned knot of bruises in action.

Imagine that you and the horse share a common skin, the classic book *Centered Riding*, by Sally Swift, tells me. Imagine, Swift says, that both of your legs have been hacked off below the knees and you're riding only with your thighs, a spry amputee, balanced evenly and spread wide in the saddle. Imagine you're a thirty-five-year-old woman, driving up to Mill Creek Equestrian Center, through the dry auburn canyons of Topanga, California, trying to recover a common skin: that ghost limb that was your life in India. That was you, at seven, centered and lean, cantering a white mare named Kara (your favorite horse) over a two-foot jump, or the chestnut Koldana, or the grey Arabian Kumal, always with the green ringneck parakeets and metronomic *wock-wock* of the coppersmith barbets in the acacias. Always with the patient calls of the instructor Raju—"Up, down! Up, down!"—hovering above the kicked-up dust, the blur of his beet-colored Sikh turban in the center of the ring.

. . . .

My parents moved overseas during the second half of the 1970s, when my father worked variously for UNICEF, a German plastic pipe manufacturing plant, the health sciences division of the International Development Research Centre, and the World Bank. They shed their Mississippi accents sometime between their moves from Dhaka to Kuala Lumpur, from Peine, Germany, to Ottawa, and finally to northern Virginia, where I was born. When they returned to Dhaka, in June of 1981, I was seven months old. We spent five years of my childhood there, and the next two in New Delhi. Listening to their voices on old Christmas videos, no one would guess my mother grew up a folk-singing Southern belle in the suburbs of Jackson, or my father a skinny bibliophile amid the gritty kudzu of Greenwood. Listening to my own now-extinct childhood dialect, I sound, at times, like a prim English schoolgirl during the era of the British Raj. "Say, Rebecca," I announce to my little sister in the video. I'm wearing a green velvet jumper over a stingray-sized ivory pinafore, and I'm holding my right pointer finger straight up beneath the branches of our synthetic pine. "Shall we?" I ask my mother, waving a wrapped present. "Yes, quite," I answer my father, with a rolling upper-crust warble. At one point, Rebecca croons to her new dolls, like the world's tiniest fairy godmother, as she tucks them into an imagined bed: "Now, now, my little ones, don't you peek out." Although neither of my parents used such antiquated expressions, we'd picked them up from the fairy tales my mother read to us—"The Necklace of Princess Fiorimonde," "Rumpelstiltskin," "Baba Yaga." All of the books she bought at Zeenat Book Supply were imported from the UK, including the six Faber volumes for children edited by Sara and Stephen Corrin. For the first eight years of my life, I spoke an exaggerated British English, a fastidious Grimm creole. *No, I shan't apologize to Rebecca because she's a wicked girl!*

Much of our lives in South Asia evokes the specter of a colonial empire: the private social club for expats; the English riding lessons; the ruffled Edwardian-style frocks that seem ripped from a tintype; the footman we referred to as "our bearer, Stephen"; the Bengali cook, David, to whom I took my first steps, and whom my mother taught how to fry chicken; the young Garo *aaya*, Onani, who helped care for Rebecca and me; the wrinkled gardener, Tota, who helped me catch frogs during monsoon season. Because of the soggy tropical heat, my mother filled our closets mostly with delicate cotton dresses instead of pants, many of them in pastel blues, yellows, creams, or mint greens, sometimes trimmed in eyelet lace or embroidered by a local tailor. The velveteen or silk ribbons my mother tied in our strawberry-blond hair—which in the moist air would spiral in frizzled ringlets—made us look like old-fashioned porcelain dolls. And our Irish complexions—ivory skin, sandy freckles, stark veins in the blue bends of our elbows—regularly fascinated Indian children unused to seeing folks without much melanin. They'd sometimes dart up to us among the clustered marigolds at Nehru Park and quickly pinch our cheeks before my mother could tug us away.

. . . .

To enhance your stability while riding a horse, imagine, suggests Sally Swift, "that your legs are growing longer, so long that your feet are resting on the ground—ground that is soft, warm summer mud." During my first riding lesson as an adult, I rode a brown buckskin pony named Snidely, who enjoyed gnawing on pepper trees, cutting corners in the ring, and trotting as slowly as possible. Even though my instructor, Jenna, hoped (I presumed) to mini-mize the distance between my rusty ass and the ground, I couldn't "grow" my calves or sink my ankles down to the mud. My limbs felt locked in place. I couldn't "open" my hip joints, my heels hung hard as rubber, and my rigid calf muscles had all the flexibility of dried corncobs. "I feel like I can't make my legs do anything," I said, trying to conceal my frustration. I used to soar on Kara through the goddamned air! Now I couldn't even hold a jumping position for more than three seconds without quivering miserably and thudding to the cantle like an amateur. Now my thighs sat like chicken cinched in plastic wrap, passive and raw. "Don't be such a perfectionist!" Jenna cried, frowning as I attempted to correct my moves en route. "Perfectionist? I've never heard that before," I deadpanned. "You have the muscle memory," she said. "It's just going to take a while to recover what you already know."

. . . .

But what about all I can't recover? I'm fine with the loss of my musty British English funneled in from the dark forests of the

Brothers Grimm. I identify as (and sound like) a Virginian, and no one in the twenty-first century says "shan't." And I embraced, ages ago, my Americanized spelling. No more *colour, centre, inflexion,* or *practise.* No more *clamour, agonise, lustre,* or *mould. Grey* remains my lone Anglophile holdout. That *a* doesn't splash a single atom of any particular color in my mind's eye: when I look at the word *gray,* I see something like an empty crawlspace in my skull. Grey with an *e* contains tiered monsoon clouds, dirty steps into stone tombs, Kumal's graceful slate flanks. As a writer, though, I mourn the cultural attack on my stylized childhood handwriting—an act I find, even now, bewildering and unforgivable.

In my first-grade class at the International School in New Delhi, I learned to write in the elegant style called D'Nealian: a fluid hybrid of print and cursive in which each letter remains separate from its neighbor but contains an ornamental flourish often nicknamed a "monkey tail" by linguists. Every letter loops a curlicue or two, like the end of a ribbon shaved to a curl with a scissors' open blade, even the unlikely e's, t's, and o's. I don't know which enforcer of American norms decided to have me "unlearn" D'Nealian. Was it my teacher in Fairfax, Virginia, when, due to my young age, I entered the American school system by repeating the second grade? Was it the principal? Was it the guidance counselor worried about culture shock, who suggested, via moose puppet, that I try wearing jeans like the other students, instead of dresses? Perhaps they felt, as others have argued, that D'Nealian creates a wasteful, unnecessary "step" between block printing and cursive, or maybe they objected to having to acclimate to grading homework penned in an alien font. So I learned to chop off my letters' whimsical monkey tails, each one a miniature Anne Boleyn, my handwriting haunted—for years—by phantom limbs. When I sift through the old schoolwork my mother saved from India, the baroque pages of my D'Nealian exercises look like an archive of correspondence compiled by some anonymous Victorian scrawler with a stutter. *Neighbour. Neighbour. Neighbour. Flavour. Flavour. Flavour.*

. . . .

The reason my grilled asparagus tasted like a hay-layered stable may be simple. I'd just come from Mill Creek. I'd brushed the dusty, sweaty Snidely. I hadn't changed out of my dark-olive jodh-purs and black boots before entering the French bistro. I can com-partmentalize the sensory scramble: Grassy shoots simulate hay straws. Sea salt recalls pony sweat. A charred vegetable dries into a smoky hide, a braid of hard leather between my teeth. I can psy-choanalyze the synesthesia: a burst of wishful earnestness toward my inner child. As I sat on my sore ass and battered thighs in the restaurant, I began to recognize a twinge of my similarly injured nostalgia. I thought of the haunted, sinuous poem by Beckian Fritz Goldberg, "Retro Lullaby," which begins, "Sometimes I carry the smell of moist hay from my childhood. / And sometimes I put down this burden, never / without its consent." A few stanzas later, Goldberg concretizes the specter of her speaker's childhood self:

> And now all I have is a postcard of a little stranger.
> If I drop the card in the hay-smell,
>
> her ear will plump up like a dried apricot in wine.
> And her stupid white hands will come up like two
>   white pages from the bottom of a lake
>
> And I'll coo, It's ok, you can be my baby.
>   My part.

Aging, Goldberg suggests, doesn't just betray our bodies; vast physiological and perceptual changes estrange us from the sense of ourselves as children. Who is that "little stranger" staring back from the family photograph? It's as if she's sent us a "postcard" from her phantasmagoric, and impossibly ongoing, adventures in the exotica of the past. Goldberg also implies that the act of remembering ("If I drop the card in the hay-smell") can reconstitute the parched body of the past, though perhaps only a fragment at a time, an organ ("her ear will plump up like a dried apricot in wine"). The speaker claims a tender, if partial, relationship between her adult and child selves: "my baby. / My part."

....

Sally Swift employs the term "soft eyes" to describe how a rider should modulate her gaze in the saddle. While "hard eyes" isolate the sharp outlines, colors, and densities of objects (Snidely's tawny ears shaped like Scotch bonnets, the drooping evergreen back-scratchers of the California pepper, the black rectangle of my husband's cell phone recording my canter), soft eyes embrace the wide scope of peripheral vision, permitting more of the world to swirl by even as you glance at a curve or an oncoming jump. "Let the object be the general center of your gaze," Swift instructs, "but look at it with your peripheral vision taking in the largest possible expanse, above and below as well as to the left and right." Details, when one uses soft eyes, whiz past in an impressionistic flux—not a blurry onslaught, but sun-dappled and supple: a rollick through the painted pastels of Monet's haystacks. Paradoxically, the more a rider takes in with her peripheral vision, the more acutely she's able to perceive the singular shape and weight of her seat—her butt and thighs—draped lightly over the saddle.

I'd like to be able to direct my soft eyes toward my childhood in South Asia, to conjure more of the periphery—more moments climbing the iron monkey bars built in front of the schoolyard's massive banyan, or passing the domed Mughal relic of Safdarjung's tomb—but I fear the false nostalgias of implanted details. I've stared at photographs and a video of myself cantering in the cracked-mud ring at Delhi Riding Club so often that I can't tell many of my memories of horseback riding in India from the images captured by the camera. Do I really remember the gentle timbre of Raju's voice or the patchy black wires of his beard or his burgundy turban, or have I created, with my hard eyes and through the easy hyperrealism of technology, a simulacrum? Is that flash of Dafadar Ji—the skinny, bent groom in his eighties who lived through Partition—real or recreated?

I have a few memories I know, most likely, are my own. They don't show up in the video, photos, or my mother's stories. There's the muscular white horse with a grey snout, Bull Bull, who had hilarious fits of rhythmic farting and would often emit a rubbery, flapping toot when my butt touched down on the saddle during a posting trot. There's the quick teakettle burst of hot horse breath when Kara curled her lips back to accept my flat-palmed offering of chopped carrots. There's the dressage move that involved making the horse prance backward. There's the time during a trust-building exercise in which I lay my head on my bareback horse's rump as I stretched my spine against her spine—finding that common skin—and stared up at the white New Delhi sky. There's the day I nearly fell from a horse (I don't recall which one) when I was first learning how to jump, and, had my mother witnessed the near catastrophe, she'd have never allowed me to return to my lessons. (The waiting area for parents was a circle of wicker chairs in the dirt near the stable, obscured from the ring.) I knew I needed to rise from the saddle in my "jumping seat," lean forward, stick my butt out like a jockey, and hold the position over the jump, but I came down too quickly (or lost my balance) and bounced hard off the saddle. I fell sideways, like a top-heavy engagement ring slipping toward its neighboring knuckle, and dangled from one stirrup, upside down, until the horse slowed and Raju raced over.

I also recall Raju leading us, a line of helmeted children on horseback, on a walk outside the razor-wire fence of Delhi Riding Club and into the teeming street, which was a sunlit jigsaw of rickshaws, honking cars, gaunt cows, beggars, and gauzy *salwar kameez*. My most vivid experience of India, beyond the high walls of my family's white stucco house and pink dahlias, is that moment in the heat, noise, and scramble of the street.

. . . .

During my second riding lesson at Mill Creek, my horse Roanie, a strawberry roan, kept halting at a certain spot toward the far left curve of the oval ring, jerking his head to the side as if he'd spotted a rattlesnake or a swarm of bees. I couldn't see anything alarming beneath the pepper trees. Jenna urged me to "be more alpha" and keep him going. "Left rein! Left rein!" she called. I tugged the outside rein. The next time around, Roanie stopped, once again, and looked intently to the side. "Left rein! Left rein!" I signaled with the rein and gave his flanks a squeeze with my ankles. Instead of picking up the trot, Roanie spooked, lurching forward and down as if he'd slipped on a banana peel. He crossed his front legs jerkily, like a break-dancer, and staggered sideways until he found his footing and hurried away from the spot that had frightened him. Instead of imagining myself as one of those legless, clown-faced, round-bottomed, wooden "roly-poly" dolls that automatically right themselves when pushed over (another of Swift's colorful visualization techniques), I hunched and cringed in the saddle, balling the reins into one panicked fist while I groped the edge of Roanie's pommel with the other, muttering, "Whoa, whoa."

Jenna rushed over. "You went fetal," she observed. "A natural response." I glanced down at Roanie's sweaty, twitching neck. "But upright forward motion is always the safest motion," she said. "That way, you have better balance." I asked Jenna why Roanie had spooked. Did he see a snake or coyote in the brush? Hear distant traffic echo down the canyon? Startle easily? "Horses are like children," she said. "They sometimes imagine things and freak themselves out."

In the section devoted to the correct use of breath in *Centered Riding*, Swift emphasizes the importance of a rider's relaxed breathing from the diaphragm. Holding your breath, even for a few seconds, causes tension in the body and can make a horse uneasy. "You can breathe a horse to quietness," Swift writes. "You can breathe him past things that scare him. If you hold your breath as you come to that big rock, he'd say, 'She's frightened! There must be gremlins there.'" Did I breathe weirdly and invent a gremlin that leaped through the pepper trees? Does Roanie now know me as a dabbler in equine hoodoo, capable of conjuring a ghost?

. . . .

Each time I watch myself riding Kara in the video taken in June 1988, I see a ghost. I look at a photograph, that "postcard of a little stranger," and see a seven-year-old girl who spins archaic turns of phrase, whose chin juts out pre-braces. I see a girl whose lavish handwriting loops monkey tails across the page. I hear Raju call my name. I watch myself round the bend in the saffron ring, Kara kicking up dust, both of us slipping past the camera my mother must have been holding, until we vanish.

PROLOGUE AS PART OF THE BODY

"Guess how I spent my Halloween?" Captain Morgan asked me over the telephone. I hadn't heard his voice in nearly five years. He spoke as fast as one of his humming tattoo guns. "I spent it in a graveyard," he said, "in Salem, Massachusetts, drinking wine beside a pond with a Croatian witch!" I told him I wasn't surprised to hear it.

The last time we'd talked, Captain Morgan had sent me the text message, "Thinking of you," beneath a photograph of a granite headstone engraved with my own last name. Five years ago, a nineteenth-century graveyard in Richmond, Virginia, had brought us together. He: an artist about to leave Richmond to open a tattoo parlor in Nashville. Me: a poet fleeing a breakup in Houston and a falling out with a close friend, Lee. I believed returning to Richmond—the city in which I'd lived for most of my twenties—and renting an apartment on the grounds of my favorite cemetery would help me recover. I could get by on funds from a recent literary grant and write poems all day, I thought, gazing into a landscape of rest.

Captain Morgan had posted an ad online for the one-bedroom he needed to abandon due to his new plans: a spacious ground-floor unit in the cemetery's former caretaker's house—that grand lavender Victorian trimmed in ivory paint just inside Hollywood Cemetery's wrought-iron front gate. As I scrolled through the rental listings, I recognized the house immediately. Amid the thorny ever-greens and leaning headstones, the mansion resembled an iconic haunted house, replete with gothic spires, bay windows, scarlet drapes, and wraparound porch. When Captain Morgan opened the door of the apartment to give me a tour, his arms and neck poked from his T-shirt. My eyes moved over his tattooed skin swirled in dense sleeves of ink.

. . . .

I lived for three years with Carrick in our narrow brick row house on South Cherry Street, three blocks away from Hollywood Cem-etery. The graveyard, designed in 1847 and landscaped in the "rural style," rises on one side of the James River in a sprawl of grassy hills and foot paths clustered with its namesake's deep green holly trees, gnarl-kneed magnolias, bark-sloughing sycamores, and three-story cedars that smell like cookie dough after the rains. Between trees tilt irregular rows of ivy-draped headstones: grey or rose-pink granite and strange white soapstones carved to mimic vine-shrouded oak stumps. My favorite graves: a pair of horizontal ledger slabs marking a married couple, Jonathan and Winnifred (I called them "Johnny and Winnie"), enclosed by a low brick wall at the steep riverside edge of the cemetery. The enclave formed a rhombus-shaped balcony overlooking the parallel lines of the rail-road tracks below and the James River beyond. I'd nod to Johnny and Winnie, saying hello if no one else was around, and then hoist myself up to perch on the far wall and watch a coal train that idled beneath my feet or peer at clusters of sunbathers sprawled on flat rocks on Belle Isle across the river. Sometimes the wallop of bongo drums pulsed downwind.

Hollywood Cemetery houses an eclectic mix of regional skeletons, including a number of major figures of the Civil War–era South: Jefferson Davis, president of the Confederacy; twenty-five Confederate generals, such as J. E. B. Stuart; a number of victims of the November 1918 influenza epidemic; Virginius Dabney, editor of the *Richmond Times Dispatch* (now nicknamed the *Richmond Times Disgrace*), who wore sharkskin trousers and won a Pulitzer for his work championing civil rights; the suffragette Lila Meade Valentine; James Monroe, the fifth president of the United States, whose tomb juts up from the middle of a sort of gazebo-sized, iron birdcage; and the Irish schoolteacher William Burke, who tutored the teenaged and not-yet-famous Edgar Allan Poe. In the middle of the graveyard sit several horseshoe-shaped "whispering benches" of cool white marble designed with concave backs that amplify and channel echoes. This way, a person seated at one end of a bench can whisper into the smooth curve over her shoulder and send her voice, with perfect clarity, all the way to the ear of the person at the opposite end. Carrick and I often sat on either side of the largest whispering bench. I don't remember which messages we shunted to one another on the slope of an echo. Probably ordinary earfuls: "Can you hear me?" "Want to have lunch?" "Nice ass!" Past the whispering benches, downhill and along the snaking main asphalt road, the cemetery's private mausoleums showcase the engraved surnames of prominent families, such as the eerie "Slaughter"; others glint their windows of royal blue, topaz, and scarlet stained glass; another's rumored to house the legendary Richmond Vampire, sprung from the bloody wreckage of a caved-in railroad tunnel.

During the time Carrick and I neighbored Hollywood Cemetery, I studied poetry as an MFA student in creative writing at Virginia Commonwealth University while he completed his undergraduate music degree. In the fall, when the steamy tidewater humidity diffused into a smoky coolness, I'd carry my classmates' poems to the cemetery and sit under one of the ancient magnolias. I'd write "use 'to be' verbs sparingly" in the margins, advocating for more colorful verb choices. I'd raise an eyebrow as I paused to sip tap water from my canteen, thinking that the dead folks lying a half a dozen feet beneath me would surely be happy to employ any "to be" verb at all. And when the man who lived directly across the street from the cemetery erected a six-foot cross made out of chicken wire in his side yard (to ward off spirits, I imagined), I felt lucky to live in Richmond's ghoulishly atmospheric neighborhood, Oregon Hill, with its gritty row houses of calico brick; weedy gardens crowded with metallic pinwheels and plaster gnomes; and pocked wall that still flaunts the painted signs for the cemetery and the long-closed Victory Rug Cleaning. Oregon Hill, a small plateau situated between two ravines, is a historically working-class neighborhood whose early nineteenth-century residents were a mixture of white and African American laborers and artisans, many of whom worked at the nearby Tredegar Iron Works plant. If I sat on the warped steps of my wooden porch on Cherry Street, chatting with my anachronistic Beat-poet neighbor, on my left rolled the pleasantly lukewarm James River and the lush hills of Hollywood Cemetery. Behind me lay other shaded streets named for local trees—Laurel, Pine—and now inhabited by rowdy students, an array of English and painting professors, and several Oregon Hill stalwarts such as the musician Apple Butter—known for engaging in fistfights with himself—and the city sanitation worker Poopy. There even lingered a few remaining descendants of folks who had moved to the neighborhood to be closer to inmates housed in the now defunct Virginia Penitentiary. To my right spread the campus of VCU and the offices of my mentors, their shelves in Anderson House filled with books. Or, as the alt-country band the Cowboy Junkies maps the ambivalent borders of the neighborhood in its bluesy, languorous tune "Oregon Hill":

> A river to the south to wash away all sins
> A college to the east of us to learn where sin begins
> A graveyard to the west of it all
> Which I may soon be lyin' in

No matter how far away I get from Richmond—whether it's the years I spent slogging through my PhD in the swamp and concrete of Houston, Texas, or ambling the jasmine-sweetened beaches of Venice, California, where I now live with my husband, David—it will always be my home. Anyplace else ends up feeling rootless and blanched, alarmingly ahistorical. I couldn't wait to leave Richmond, actually. After eight years, I was ready to leave. But since I've left town, I've realized that Richmond, for better or worse, will always haunt me. Its slow, brown river and abandoned ironworks plant. Its horrifying past ties to the slave trade. Its corner diner with the walls mottled with collages and bisque doll heads. It's where all my own ghosts lie. My two ex-boyfriends: Ed, the glassblower-Deadhead who went to jail for selling pot; Carrick, the jazz-and-bluegrass bassist who returned to Appalachia. My former apartments: the flophouse on Grove with my sewing machine perched on the ash-covered coffee table; the one-bedroom on Hanover with the perilous blue balcony; the place on Park in which my fashion-design-major roommate knitted a quasi-Victorian bustle of bulging tea roses she called, gloriously,

"Butt Garden"; the row house on Cherry, the street next to which the dead and I slept equally well.

. . . .

In his 1936 essay "The Storyteller," Walter Benjamin argues that the decline of the artisan class has imperiled the art of storytelling. The "two archaic types" of storytellers are, Benjamin suggests, "the resident tiller of the soil" (the farmer who stays put and nourishes local folklore and regional history) and "the trading seaman" (the journeyman who travels to distant places and returns with exotic tales). Storytelling relies on the art of repetition, Benjamin notes, and the art of telling erodes when "the gift for listening is lost and the community of listeners disappears." "It is lost," Benjamin writes:

> because there is no more weaving and spinning to go on while they are being listened to. The more self-forgetful the listener is, the more deeply is what he listens to impressed upon his memory. When the rhythm of work has seized him, he listens to the tales in such a way that the gift of retelling them comes to him all by itself. This, then, is the nature of the web in which the gift of storytelling is cradled. This is how today it is becoming unraveled at all its ends after being woven thousands of years ago in the ambience of the oldest forms of craftsmanship.

I like to imagine Captain Morgan as one of Walter Benjamin's archetypal yarn-spinners, a contemporary artisan tapped into the intricate rhythms of his craft, crouched over someone's exposed skin as he weaves his stories to the drone of a needle. He'd once told an especially forgetful client to call him "Captain Morgan," instead of "Morgan," as a mnemonic. As the man recommended the tattoo artist's services to friends, repeating the nickname, the moniker spread throughout Richmond, eventually prompting a legal name change. "It took on a life of its own," Captain Morgan said. He told me he believes people seek to be marked by his ink due to an ancient impulse, a tribal instinct: "People come to me looking for something old."

. . . .

"I talk a lot," Captain Morgan said, laughing, over the phone, "so my friend the Croatian witch told me to be quiet for a minute so we could just drink our wine by the pond." I'm reminded of the stories Captain Morgan told me during our one—and only—in-person exchange in Richmond. Over scrambled eggs and mimosas, he asked me to recite a poem. Here was someone who didn't care that I'd cheated on my boyfriend of seven years with a poet twice my age, humiliated Carrick by the gossip that ensued, lost one of my best friends, Lee, who was also my most important literary mentor, and felt so wrecked by shame, shock, and a lacerating, self-aimed rage that all I could think to do was to vanish back into Richmond, where I'd once felt safe. I would change my story. I wouldn't be the girl who dragged her boyfriend from Richmond to Houston, a place we both immediately loathed. I wouldn't have sobbed in a bathroom stall in the middle of my dissertation defense, hoping someone—an undergraduate, a custodian, a professor from another department—would comfort me. I wouldn't have tearfully confessed my circumstance to a Boston architect at a bistro bar in George Bush Intercontinental Airport, my black cat yowling from a mesh pet carrier in my lap. As I sat in the booth across from Captain Morgan in Richmond, I felt seen in a way that I hadn't in a long time. My scandal had eclipsed my ability to focus on my writing and redefined several of my most important relationships, including the one I had with myself. Was I a bad person? Sociopathic? At least I wasn't a murderer, although at times I'd felt like one.

. . . .

The Hebrew Bible's first recorded murderer, Cain, bears an indelible mark on his body often perceived as a symbol of his grievous sin. According to the Book of Genesis, however, after Cain slays his brother Abel and God banishes him from the land, Cain confesses to the Lord his fear that someone might murder him during his travels. In her essay "How to Read a Tattoo, and Other Perilous Quests," scholar Juniper Ellis writes: "Cain protests that in his wanderings 'anyone may kill me at sight.' 'Not so!' declared the Lord, and 'put a mark on Cain, lest anyone should kill him at sight' (see Genesis 4:1—16)." "In other words," Ellis notes, "the so-called mark of Cain, a tattoo, is as much a sign of God's protection as it is an indication of the wearer's having committed fratricide." Paradoxically cast off from and protected by the divine, Cain must wander the earth, searching for meaning in his life.

. . . .

"Tattooing is an ancient profession," Captain Morgan continued. "It's an extension of ourselves, of self." I asked him to tell me the story of his own first tattoo: a design based on a pattern of lizards he'd hallucinated during his debut LSD trip. "It's a timeless pattern," he said, one that he can summon, even now, without the help of acid. "It's a kind of visual language." Originally, a famous Swiss tattoo artist who'd planned to be in Manhattan for three days was supposed to give Captain Morgan his lizard tattoo. Stuck in Virginia, however, Captain Morgan couldn't make any of the dates, so the artist put him on the waitlist of an associate who tattooed people out of a house on the Lower East Side. Captain Morgan wavered for several days before he finally decided to make the trip. "I felt like I was in a movie," he said of his bus ride from rural Lynchburg to New York City. He was nineteen and it was his first time riding a Greyhound. In the 1990s, he recalled, the Lower East Side resembled the Wild West: crack-related violence plagued the streets and, because of the AIDS epidemic, tattooing was illegal in the city. Captain Morgan found his way from the Greyhound station to the tattoo artist's house, arriving several hours early to discover the place packed with other clients. The artist led Captain Morgan to the front stoop, pointed toward a dive bar across the street, and said to wait there, warning him, "Do *not* go anywhere."

When Captain Morgan returned to the house for his appointment, he noticed the artist spoke at least five languages. Stories spilled from the man as if in counterpoint to the buzzing rhythms of the tattoo gun: he told an anecdote in Portuguese to his wife, and other tales in French, Italian, English, and Spanish to various clients, who continued to drop by throughout the night. "He looked like a pirate!" Captain Morgan said, remembering the artist's crowded mouthful of gold teeth. "It was my first step into another world," he added, and it's this sense of transformation he hopes his own clients will experience.

Back at the Greyhound station, post-tattoo, Captain Morgan looked around the packed waiting area and noticed someone drawing on a sketchpad. He felt drawn to the person—short-haired, slender, androgynous. "Even if it turned out to be a guy," he said, "I'm on board. I'm not afraid of that." The person turned out to be Maria, a world-traveling welder who'd returned to New York after a stint in India during which she worked side by side with Mother Teresa, washing, as she termed it, "homeless women's butts." Mother Teresa encouraged Maria to go back to her old city and share all that she'd learned. As Captain Morgan glanced down at Maria's drawing, he noticed she'd arranged his face and those of the other waiting passengers in rows across the page, like one of those tiered group portraits of elementary schoolkids. "We had this amazing moment," he said. Although they didn't stay in touch, he'd always remembered her story.

．．．．．．．．．．．

"I've talked about you so much," Captain Morgan told me when he called after five years. "Our magical cemetery story!" I loved that we'd become familiar characters in each other's tales: two artists who'd converged at transitional times, united at first through Hollywood Cemetery, and then through a recognition of our similar taste for strange stories and love of poetry. Whitman and Ginsberg were his "gateway poets," he'd confided, and he also loved the work of Ted Hughes, especially the dark fables in *Crow*. Captain Morgan remembered asking me to recite a poem as we sat in the café. I chose Beckian Fritz Goldberg's "Prologue as Part of the Body," a hypnotic poem that evokes the onset of death as a beguiling conflation of the senses—a deadly synesthesia brought on by an erotic waft of some *femme fatale*'s flower, à la Billie Holiday's trademark gardenia:

> It begins with something backward—
> gardenia tucked behind
> the ear as if scent could hear
> its undoing
>
> the fantastic bodice of a space
> no larger than this plump
> of sweetness, yeastlike, tropic

it begins with a turning, a trope,
that fragrance spiraling the cochlea
and the body confused by the enchantment
of the wrong orifice wrong passage—it was

after all where music should be unwinding,
cry shedding its epithelial layers, the tac-tac
of someone entreating, far away, some door . . .

But it was summer trying to enter, swoon its way
into the skull, the Parfum Fatale collapsing
on the organ of Corti

a secret island discovered by the Italian anatomist
of the last century though it was always there
in the body, the locus of quivering
like the letter M

deep in its alphabet, the humming
on either side. Beginning is

the flower to the car
the flute to the palm, the glittering mirror to
the back of the head, the steaming rice and the plums
in honey

to the feet, to the vertebrae, to the pineal gland:

oblivion, oblivion, oblivion.

At the time, I hadn't told Captain Morgan that only two weeks earlier I'd come close to choosing oblivion. That before I moved back to Virginia I'd called a suicide hotline in Houston and confessed my plans to a stranger. I imagined a great release, a freedom as death moved through my limbs and spine until it finally reached the mythical location of the soul—"to the feet, to the vertebrae, to the pineal gland." I was grateful to have changed my mind, grateful for the willing listeners. The entire time I recited the Goldberg poem, Captain Morgan leaned forward, chin propped on his hands, nodding. He gushed, when I was done, "I could tell you were tasting the words."

. . . .

Neither my husband David nor I have any tattoos. If I'd gotten the one I'd envisioned, at nineteen, I'd have a scene from J. R. R. Tolkien's *The Hobbit* inking my entire back: the green hills of the Shire, dotted with hairy-footed hobbits. All three of my previous boyfriends had tattoos. My high school boyfriend, Chris, a longhaired metalhead who became a junkie, had hand-poked *OZZY* across the knuckles of his left hand. My undergraduate boyfriend, Ed, had a stuttering black spiral that began at his right armpit and coiled above his nipple like a fiddlehead fern. My grad school boyfriend, Carrick, had two tattoos. The first one portrayed his self-designed symbol of order and chaos: the quadratic equation in which all of the letters and numbers in the formula were rendered in crisp black ink, with the exception of X. The unknown figure, waiting to be solved, was engulfed in wavy orange flames. His second tattoo, which he'd gotten toward the end of our time in Houston in honor of his master's degree in bass performance and pedagogy, depicted the "circle of fifths": a geometrical representation of the relationships between the twelve tones of the chromatic scale, their corresponding key signatures, and the related major and minor keys. The image looked like an evenly sliced-up pie garnished with musical symbols. Once, during a long-ago cemetery walk in Richmond, Carrick brought his fiddle with us so he could play the musical notes we'd noticed, during a previous stroll, engraved on a large headstone. The first time we'd seen the grave, fiddle-less, he'd stood in front of the granite, sight-reading and humming the tune as he swayed and tapped his right foot. The next time, he'd lifted his instrument and bowed the strings, filling the ryegrass and magnolias with the dead music lover's requested hymn.

....

Captain Morgan gave his Croatian witch-friend Vesna her first tattoo several Halloweens ago as she lay on top of her kitchen table in Salem, Massachusetts. As Vesna rested her head on a pillow, he tattooed a simple wing behind one of her ears as her roommate watched. Afterward, she and her friend left town, and Captain Morgan found himself walking aimlessly around Salem, aching from a sudden loneliness. "I could feel a chasm," he recalled, "when they were gone." He reached the wharf, gazing at ships in the distance and, as he walked, the echoes of his footsteps inspired him to write a song for Vesna. "It was written," he said, "by the space they'd left behind." The next time he saw Vesna, Captain Morgan gave her a traditional Japanese *kanji* tattoo and, afterward, sang her the footstep song, a cappella, holding her as they both wept. Next, she gave him a tattoo: the hand-poked letters *VY*, which entwined to form the initials of her nickname, "Ves Yes."

The hand-poke tattoos that Captain Morgan gives and receives feel the most meaningful, he told me, because he gets "fired up by the connection with the other person." "They're less subject-oriented and more interpersonal," he said. One of his hand-poke designs was given to him by his then-girlfriend: the date of a particular Halloween they spent together in Salem. Another hand-poke image maps the craggy lapis outline of the Blue Ridge Mountains, which his friend Camilla had designed for herself. After he'd finished her tattoo, he said, "We're not done," and she stared at him, waiting. "Now you're going to do me." I asked him if his tattoos—the old girlfriend's hand-poked date, Vesna's initials, Camilla's mountain range, the vision of lizards, the whimsical carrot on his right ankle done (with his guidance) by a Belgian metalhead in the medieval city of Ghent—began to speak to one another, if tattoo artists create a larger, continuous story on the skin. "Yes," he said, pausing, "but we begin by blindly stumbling into it. Like writers, people with tattoos have to find their voice."

. . . .

"The storytelling that thrives for a long time in the milieu of work," writes Walter Benjamin, "—the rural, the maritime, and the urban—is itself an artisan form of communication, as it were." "It does not aim to convey the pure essence of the thing," he continues, "like information or a report. It sinks the thing into the life of the storyteller, in order to bring it out of him again. Thus traces of the storyteller cling to the story the way the handprints of the potter cling to the clay vessel."

. . . .

I was a potter for half of my eight years in Richmond. My ceramics teacher, Steve, a lanky red-bearded Wisconsinite in his late thirties, taught me how to throw pots on the wheel. As one of the final touches before I cut the still-wet vessel from the wheel head, he showed me how to leave a mark on the bottom interior of the form by gently pressing my right thumb into the clay as I spun the wheel around once, leaving a spiral, a distinctive ridge-like swirl. This way, each time someone finished her coffee and glanced down into the empty mug, she'd be reminded of the artist's touch at the center of the object.

Steve also taught me how to "pull" handles from a lump of moist clay shaped like an eggplant. I'd hold the fat end in my right hand, dip the fingers of my left hand in a pitcher of water, and repeatedly pull the tapered bulb outward and down, maintaining even pressure, thinning and narrowing the ribbon of clay until I'd shaped a six- or seven-inch-long handle. Before severing the ribbon from the rest of the lump, I'd give it one last slow pull, running my thumb down the center in order to create a smooth shallow for a future coffee drinker to comfortably rest her own thumb. When the handle dried enough to hold its shape, I'd score the two ends with a pin tool and press them into the vessel, leaving, as Steve taught me, the impression of my thumb at the top and bottom of the handle, where each part joined the mug's body.

Although I've kept dozens of my own handmade pots from art school, I prefer to drink my morning coffee from Steve's mugs. It's how I remain close to him. It's how I recall his Wisconsin drawl each time he'd greet me, poking his head into the ceramics studio as I threw at the wheel ("Hey, Eee-a-nuh!"), or his love for his black lab Gerstley (named after Gerstley Borate, an ingredient used to mix glazes), who'd cringe behind Steve's toilet during thunderstorms, or that night I went with Steve and a few of his grad students to see a funk band in Bogart's smoky back room (an ex-speakeasy) and we all danced. Even though I haven't seen Steve since he left VCU when I was twenty-one, I can press my thumb into the ghost print of his nearly fifteen years later and find a phantom fit. I can sit, here in California, sipping my coffee, and feel the shape of my former life.

. . . .

Curious about what it would be like to leave a mark on a person and map a story on someone's skin, I bought a pair of tattoo guns and a set of twenty inks. I also ordered some synthetic "practice skins": a ten-pack of six-by-eight-inch rectangles of beige-colored rubber. They looked like pot holders made from human pelts that might hang on the kitchen wall of a gingerbread house inhabited by an evil fairy tale witch. The guns—one with a metallic red grip and the other blue—came in Ziplocs filled with dozens of unassembled parts, an instructional CD-ROM, in Chinese, and a list of eleven oddly translated "tattoo guidelines," in English, that seemed by turns menacing (number three: "Heart disease: will stimulate cause seizures"), apocryphal (number six: "Woman's menstrual period: poor immunity"), and accidentally metaphysical (number eight: "Spirit is not normal or has a history of spirit: will affect the disease").

After David and I watched an amateur instructional video on YouTube, we assembled our guns and sketched our designs. Mine: a simplified outline of a fox. I planned to fill in the body with decorative swirls that resembled the curlicues of wrought-iron gates. David's initial design: an elaborate still life of a bowl filled with grapes, pears, apples, and a banana. He soon realized the image was far too large and detailed for a novice and instead tattooed a cartoon June bug across the canvas of his practice skin. I chose light brown ink for my fox, surprised at the difficulty of maintaining continuous lines. My hands shook as if from delirium tremens, even when I turned the pulsating gun's power down to half speed. And when I filled in the small triangles of the animal's ears, watching the needle repeatedly prick the fake skin, I realized I was flinching in sympathy with my phantom client. When I finished my fox, the animal recalled a wobbly organic design squeezed from a tube of dry, clotted henna. "I have," I declared, jabbing my gun in the air, "a new respect for the line." Finally, when I flipped over my synthetic skin to expose a jagged two-inch rip, I realized that had this been the skin of a real person, my vibrating needle, on which I pressed too heavily, might've pierced down and hit the bone.

. . . .

I've learned the Japanese word for the border area between tattooed and non-tattooed areas of the skin: *mikiri*. There are a number of techniques of *mikiri*, each one resulting in a different style, shape, and shading on the skin: a certain visual quality of division. *Matsuba mikiri* ("pine-needle border") demarcates a spiky gestural edge, like the bristled outline of a pine tree. *Botan mikiri* ("tree-peony border") creates a scalloped border, like an undulant row of round peony petals. *Butsugiri* ("line border") maintains a clean, straight border, an unbroken line. *Akebono mikiri* ("dawn border") evokes the bruised margins of a sunrise: that smudged horizon between sky and land, ink and skin.

. . . .

After Captain Morgan moved to Nashville, we lost touch. And after I moved into his apartment on the grounds of Hollywood Cemetery, I realized that without his magnetic presence and colorful tales, I felt alone in Richmond. Although I wasn't frightened of living in the cemetery, even at night, I realized I was the one—and not the holly thickets or mossy stones—who was haunted. Each time I stood within the three-foot chill of my panoramic bay windows, I glimpsed a different ghost. Some days it was my estranged poetry mentor, Lee, walking with me down the sloping road of Hollywood Cemetery past the groundskeeper's house. We'd once run into a fiction professor crouched in the grass, stooping to snap photographs. "I'm taking pictures of fungi," she'd sputtered, blinking rom behind her glasses. We'd walked off, nudging each other. Other days I could almost see Carrick's auburn beard breezing from the bark of the peeling cedars. Sometimes even the wind brought with it the splintered notes of that moment he taught me how to play "Somewhere Over the Rainbow" with a horsehair bow on the toothless edge of his singing saw. I sounded like a preschool violinist—all squeaks and sharps and flats. And why hadn't I considered that his ancestral plot was here—a whole population of headstones engraved with his Scots-Irish family names—that loomed on the hill in their grey judgment as if to convey, in unison, *You're unforgivable.*

The hardest part of my return to Richmond, though, was feeling haunted by the living present. Lee, who wasn't speaking to me, lived only two blocks away. The tattooed server at 821 Café asked one day, as she dropped off my brunch check, if I'd seen my friend sitting at the counter. "The one you're always here with who orders the Earl Grey and omelet with spinach and bacon. I thought it was weird," she added, "that he left without saying hi." Later that evening, after I'd been pacing the apartment, nervous about my phone interview for a university teaching position the next morning, I'd accidentally locked myself out when I went to check the mail. My new front door, heavier than I was used to, had shut and locked automatically. I was in my pajamas, without a coat, and about five inches of snow covered the ground. It was still snowing. No one else in the groundskeeper's house appeared to be home, though I could hear an upstairs TV. No one answered my knocks. The fact that I couldn't even walk two blocks to Lee's to borrow his phone made me sink to the boards of the front porch in tears. I finally trekked the four blocks to the café, where one of the owners gave me a mug of steaming peppermint tea on the house and a server handed me her cell phone. An hour later, a cab took me to my landlord's house and back to the graveyard, where I used the spare key. The next morning my voice shook throughout the phone interview—not from my coatless wanderings in the snow but because by then I knew I couldn't stay. I was friendless, in a winter graveyard, my magnificent apartment entirely wasted on me: a poet who couldn't write, the rangy days without shape or purpose. If the borders of my self were shaded in ink, they'd form the blue slur of the *akebono mikiri*, blurring my past with my present, my hope with my burden. My green landscape of rest now shone, hard and featureless, in snow.

. . . .

After five nights alone in the graveyard, I abandoned the apartment and, at thirty years old, moved in with my parents and younger sister, in Fairfax, an hour and a half north. Rebecca had recently graduated with her master's degree in Oral History from Columbia University and, priced out of her place in Brooklyn and unable to find a job, returned for nine months to our childhood house. Our circumstances at first seemed similar: I'd received my doctorate from the University of Houston and I, too, was unemployed and needed to come home. I spent most of the months I lived at my parents' house lying in bed with my cat, crying in the middle of dinner as my parents looked on helplessly, or hiking around the nearby suburban pond with my mother. Rebecca busied herself reposting the photographs of my ex that I'd un-tacked from the kitchen bulletin board—to show her solidarity with Carrick—and mailing a series of anonymous envelopes to her former roommate in New York. Each envelope contained a single pewter murder weapon—a knife, revolver, candlestick, wrench, or lead pipe—that she'd removed from the murder-mystery board game *Clue*. "Do you think I should start with the wrench," she asked me, "and then follow it with the candlestick, and arrange them according to their increasing level of menace?" I realized that we were both uniquely broken.

. . . .

Five years later, Rebecca was living in Copenhagen and conducting research for her anthropology dissertation while I'd gotten a teaching job in Los Angeles. We both referred to our postgraduate disasters as "the dark year." Although Lee never apologized for abandoning our friendship—or for ratting me out to Carrick for my affair—he wrote to me after I'd lived in LA for a year and a half, in part to justify his behavior yet expressing his desire to rebuild our friendship. I knew this gesture—defensive, contradictory—was as much as he'd ever be able to offer. Now, when Lee and I hang out, we bring our spouses. Instead of once a week, we speak on the phone a couple of times a year. We're not anywhere close to recovering the friendship we once shared, though this cautious incarnation does honor, I think, its long and complicated bond.

During a recent summer visit to Richmond, I went with David to an exhibit at the Virginia Museum of Fine Arts, "Japanese Tattoo: Perseverance, Art, and Tradition," where we admired roomfuls of life-sized photographs of seminude tattooed people suspended from the ceiling, the massive panels as tall as sails. Many of the photographs of the traditional Japanese tattoos, or *irezumi*, featured muscular men in full or partial bodysuits. Their backs, shoulders, buttocks, and upper thighs undulated with multicolored dragons, amber-scaled koi, curly-maned Lions of Buddha, rising phoenixes, folkloric demons, and cascades of loose fuchsia cherry blossoms. Much of the enduring imagery inflecting Japanese tattoos derives from *ukiyo-e* woodblock prints, popular from the Edo through the Meiji periods (the seventeenth through the early twentieth centuries).

Ukiyo-e—"pictures of the floating world"—remind us that all existence is transitory, as in the Zen metaphysics of the wind-tossed maple leaves, peonies, or cherry blossoms, the fragile *sakura* broken free from the branch and hovering, gradually, toward earth.

During my time as an art student at VCU, I taught a lesson on *ukiyo-e* prints to a class of elementary school children. Instead of woodblocks, I'd passed out pink rectangles cut from recycled Styrofoam lunch trays onto which the children carved—by pressing down on their dull pencil points—images of ephemerality: magnolia leaves, daisies, sunflowers, snowflakes.

. . . .

By the time of the tattoo exhibit, the many shades and layers of Richmond's ghost town seemed, at this distance, to enfold more good memories than bad. David and I met Lee at Belle Isle, the forested five-hundred-acre island (and former POW camp for Union soldiers) across the river from Hollywood Cemetery. We crossed the narrow suspension footbridge, which shook from the pounding of joggers, and dodged dog turds, pausing to watch a couple of teenage boys leap from the bridge, one after the other, into a deep part of the James. We cheered from the edge, clapping. Arriving at the island's flat rocks, we sat, the guys talking behind me as I rolled up my jeans and dangled my bare feet in the current. I could see a coal train smoking on the tracks beyond me and the many graves, white and grey, Johnny's and Winnie's, teething the leafy hills of the cemetery on the other side of the river. Kicking my legs in the water, I listened as David described the tattoo exhibit and the images of "the floating world." I kept my eyes fixed on Oregon Hill, my old neighborhood of artisans and folks who sit on their front stoops in the evenings to share stories. "[W]omen on the porches," sing the Cowboy Junkies, "comparin' alibis."

. . . .

As I revisit the tattoo exhibition's color catalogue at my home in California, I keep returning to the same image: an intricate color piece by the renowned tattoo artist Shige. The artwork ripples across the back of a nude woman who stands with her spine toward the camera, her black hair flipped over her right shoulder to better display her tattoo, whose focal point is a cavernous human skull that spans her shoulder blades. What is it about this design that keeps pulling me in? In *irezumi*, the skull is not, I've discovered, a symbol of death or danger. Instead the image prompts people to invite change into their lives, to "embrace the new." The artist Shige, however, who smiles—composed and wryly amused—from his headshot in the exhibit's catalogue, provocatively subverts the conventional symbolism of the human skull, as he covers the woman's back in crawling maggots and seaweed-like wisps that could be red hair or raw viscera. The skull's two eye sockets seem deliberately positioned—in shape, size, and location—to resemble scooped negatives of the woman's breasts, as if one could peer through her back into the live interior of her body. Fusing *irezumi* imagery with the outlaw aesthetic of biker tattoos (which Shige encountered during his early work as a mechanic for Harley-Davidson), the artist weaves an ambivalent taunt. Is this bodily landscape one of harrowing decay or teeming regeneration? Into the skull's right eye socket twists a monstrous violet centipede, which emerges, open-mouthed, from the left one. "Exactly," I thought, nodding. "I've been there."

Above the skull's cranium hover orange and white moths while below pink peonies blossom across the woman's buttocks, the edges of her tattoo dark and soft as smeared coal—the trademark of the *akebono mikiri*. The dawn border: that gradual, bruise-like blurring between ink and skin, like the cumulous edge of a sunrise, a slow transition.

RETRO ANATOMY OF A STRING BASS

During bluegrass gigs my former boyfriend Carrick, an upright bassist, used to wear a canary-yellow vintage T-shirt emblazoned with the Jujyfruits logo and the dazed face of a cartoon boy tipped toward a hovering nebula of red and green gumdrops. Carrick had bought the shirt at the Salvation Army because he found the image unintentionally psychoactive and therefore hilarious. (Those colorful candies looked like benzos, we'd agreed, and that kid's dilated pupils and daffy grin were pure whacked-out drug bliss.) He'd trimmed the bottom hem to make a cropped half-shirt, which exposed his craft-beer belly each time he raised his arms onstage to play the bass. With his auburn beard that ebbed and flowed in profile—topiaric—between the whiskers of Karl Marx and Darwin, bared hairy midriff, and leather bow quiver strapped like a gun holster to his right thigh, his stage persona was something like Britney Spears meets Yosemite Sam in a jug band. He'd dance with his string bass in time to the music, bobbing his chin as he shifted his weight from foot to foot.

Carrick owned three string basses. One he kept on campus, in the jazz department at VCU, where we were students, and two lived with us for seven years like a pair of moody roommates, alternately mute and ecstatic. We crammed our brick row house in Richmond with more instruments than most other objects (exceptions: books and records). Mandolins and fiddles perched on wall brackets, burnished and curvilinear as beetles. A herd of banjos and acoustic guitars rose from A-frame stands by the idle fireplace. Two full-size keyboards formed an "L" in the corner near the front door. There were even obscure instruments, like the theremin Carrick assembled from a Moog kit, or invented ones, like the dildo-phone: that raunchy mock trombone he made by rubber-banding a plastic kitchen funnel to a silicone dildo. But the upright basses loomed like Druids and took up most of the space. They were Carrick's favorite, his specialty.

He played an eclectic range of genres (jazz, bluegrass, old-time, big band, funk, classical, rockabilly, blues, roots) as well as in a diverse number of groups: the potty-mouthed vaudevillian octet Special Ed and the Shortbus Bluegrass Band (imagine Frank Wakefield grafted onto Frank Zappa), popular on the Richmond bar scene and hippie music festival circuit; the lounge-jazz trio for which he donned his Banana Republic suit, toned down his leprechaun kinesics, and sent "The Girl from Ipanema" purling over shrimp and grits at the Jefferson Hotel's Sunday brunch; the funk-infused gospel quartet that performed for a historic African American church and was comprised of three other VCU jazz students—all of them black—and the ruddy Scots-Irish-complected Carrick, which the guys christened Three Pieces and a Biscuit (the congregation loved the punch line).

. . . .

Double bass, contrabass, kontrabass, bass viol, and *bass violin* all name the body of the bass. Some terms distinguish the acoustic from its electric incarnation: *upright bass, standup bass, bass fiddle, string bass.* Others try to sketch—through metaphor—the hefty instrument's strange grace: *elephant, doghouse, bull fiddle, the tree.*

To me the upright bass's shape has always conjured a person's: it has parts called a head, a neck, and a belly; it possesses a back, two shoulders, and a waist. Other terms draw from the character of negative space. The concave C-bouts delineate the cinched middle of the hourglass and make room for the plunging gestures of a bow. And the pair of *f*-holes, carved on either side of the bridge like mirror-image cursive *f*'s, allow sounds to vibrate more freely from the hollow body.

Ever since Man Ray painted black *f*-holes across the gelatin silver print of Kiki de Montparnasse's nude back in 1924 and rephotographed the image to create his *Le Violon d'Ingres,* turning the female body into a violin, *f*-holes have been popular back tattoos. The tension in Man Ray's iconic surrealist photograph lies between the beauty of the classical nude and crude objectification, between seductiveness and a creeping unease, and the way the Parisian model Kiki crosses her arms in front of her chest, concealing her limbs from the camera, evokes both metamorphosis and dismemberment.

No matter how familiar I'd become with the bodies of Carrick's instruments, I'd often walk past one of his six-foot-tall string basses in the dark and mistake it for a burglar hunched in the corner. I'd gasp and knock my shin into the coffee table before shaking off the double take.

. . . .

The first time Carrick brought me to Blacksburg, his rural hometown in the mountainous southwestern tip of Virginia, we'd just adopted a three-month-old kitten and decided to bring her with us. Carrick's mother feared Jellybean would infest her house with fleas, so we stayed in the upstairs apartment of his father's orthodontist office in town: an old Victorian on Main Street. Despite Carrick's belief that the office was haunted (slamming doors, hidden toothbrushes, turned-on lights, screams from the basement), this was the more desirable sleeping arrangement. His relationship with his mother had been strained since he gave up the violin for the bass as a teenager. She'd groomed him to be a concert violinist, making three-year-old Carrick practice holding a toy fiddle with a pencil pressed against its belly like a bow, even though doing so produced no sound. She wanted him to get used to the gesture. After years of violin summer camps and weekly lessons, her youngest son's defection to the upright bass—to jazz and bluegrass and late gigs at smoky bars—was a choice she'd neither understood nor fully forgiven.

The upper floor of the orthodontist office contained a kitchen, den, bathroom, and bedroom, where Carrick's father could stay if the narrow country roads vanished in snow or whenever he needed a few days alone, away from the family. The examination rooms and waiting area for his father's patients took up the downstairs floor. Carrick had told me that many of his classmates in middle school got their braces from his dad and that plaster casts of their crooked teeth sat on shelves in a storage closet. I had asked Carrick if he ever poked around to locate the dental molds labeled with the names of girls he'd had crushes on, so he could hold parts of them in secret. I wish I could remember what he said.

We spent the night in the office's upstairs bedroom and I woke up in an unusual position, lying flat on my back, leaden from sleep paralysis. Although I couldn't turn my head or roll myself over, I could see every object in the room ripple in the sunlight as if the room were gradually filling with olive oil, while the dark slur of a figure loomed over the bed repeating: *Get out of the house. Get out of the house.* Carrick startled when I told him about the hallucination, saying he'd had an almost identical vision in the past. We decided to leave Blacksburg early.

. . . .

Carrick's parents had sent his older sister to a private Catholic girls' school in Richmond and shipped his older brother to an elite boarding school for boys in Charlottesville. Both institutions funneled a large portion of their graduates into the University of Virginia, the college (red brick buildings, neoclassical Corinthians) immodestly nicknamed "the Harvard of the South." As soon as the kids hit puberty, Carrick's parents wanted them out of the house with their loud music and adolescent drama. Carrick was the baby of the family at seven years younger than his brother and fourteen years his sister's junior. When he reached middle school, his parents expected him to go to the same rich-boy boarding school in Charlottesville and graduate from UVA, like a good prep, like his violin-playing, obedient brother. Carrick refused. Leaving Blacksburg would mean leaving his bands, his bluegrass buddies, and his avuncular mentors who'd taught him how to play real old-time music. And besides, where would he store his upright bass at a boarding school aimed at future mortgage bankers and engineers? Carrick's mother was outraged, but his father had respected his standing up for himself and allowed him to stay.

. . . .

The Purple Fiddle is a café, community gathering space, mountain market, and venue for Appalachian-based acoustic music located on a quiet stretch of Highway 32 in the leafy town of Thomas,

West Virginia. The landmark's large, violin-shaped marquee juts its purple body sideways, just above the doorway's overhang, and sports the name of the venue in wavy yellow letters beneath a painted sun. The sign is too huge to mimic a fiddle one might tuck under a chin and bow; it's closer in size to the largest instrument in the violin family, the upright bass.

I traveled with Carrick and his string bass to West Virginia several times when he and the other seven members of Special Ed and the Shortbus Bluegrass Band played at the Purple Fiddle. Zipped in its black canvas case the bass took up half of his station wagon, stretching its shoulders and neck over the flipped-forward backseat. Because the Purple Fiddle was family-friendly—swarmed with children who'd flat-foot to the music across the hardwood floors—the Shortbus guys tended to omit their naughtier numbers: the rollicking scatological chant "Who Flung Poo"; the cover of Zappa's deranged doo-wop tune "What's the Ugliest Part of Your Body?" (replete with harmonized "woo-*wee*-ooos"); and the loony satire of a birds-and-the-bees sex talk written by Carrick, "T and A," in which a serious-sounding patriarch attempts to impart to his son everything he knows about tits and ass. Not to pathologize or oversimplify Carrick's sense of humor, but I've seen in his beaming, excitable, and essentially sweet nature a keen edge of reflexive defiance, an urge toward subversion, a naughty Shakespearean sprite grinning behind an upright.

············

I wasn't in the car the night Carrick drove a few members of the Shortbus back from a gig and hit a patch of black ice. Theirs was the only car on that stretch of the highway. The five-string banjoist recounted how the station wagon spun once or twice before careening into a skid and everyone sat in terrified silence, gripping their arm rests, everyone except Carrick. He let loose a giddy "Wheeee! Wheeee!" grasping the steering wheel and tipping his head back as if thrilled by a roller coaster ride, until they finally lurched to a stop along the shoulder. I'm not sure if it was Carrick's knee-jerk insurgent clowning or visceral nervousness that inspired his reaction, but I've always thought that if I had to pick one story to capture his sensibility, it might be that slow-motion spin over black ice and toward potential death, in which Carrick's decision was automatic: choosing to make people laugh.

. . . .

I don't remember the first time I saw Carrick perform. It must've been at Richie's Pub (now defunct) on the corner of Meadow and Broad, before the Shortbus had a substantial local following. I do recall my delight at discovering that the guy who wrote and sang lead vocals on "Who Flung Poo" ("Who flung poo? / Who flung poo? / Who flung poo? / Fuck you!") also penned the wistful blue-grass tune "Each to Each," which quoted T. S. Eliot's Prufrock in the chorus: "Shall I part my hair behind? Do I dare to each a peach? / I shall wear white flannel trousers, and walk upon the beach. / I heave heard the mermaids singing, each to each." Each time Carrick stepped onstage and grabbed his bass, his mouth stretched into a goofy elastic grin, his eyes widened and rolled, his chin jutted in and out to the rhythms. As he shuffled his feet, his whole body, like his bass's, seemed to vibrate.

. . . .

The last time I saw Carrick perform we'd been broken up for a couple of months. We'd continued to live together in Houston, where we'd moved three years earlier so I could earn my PhD in creative writing and literature. We slept in separate bedrooms but met up nightly for dinner as we finished the final months of our respective graduate degrees. I think we knew that one—or both—of us might not finish up if we suddenly abandoned our routines. Over the past few years I'd watched Carrick morph from an exuberant jazz musician in VCU's robust, experimental department into a stricken MA student in bass performance and pedagogy at the University of Houston's small, conservative program. Carrick's instructors sneered at improvisatory techniques and pushed him to play mainly classical music, a period in which he felt constrained, alienated, less himself. But wasn't this the city of Lightnin' Hopkins and Barrie Lee Hall? Where the hell had I dragged Carrick? The conflict now seems an echo of that clash from fifteen years earlier, when his mother tried to mold him into a concert violinist and he rebelled, only this time he'd made the opposite decision: he'd quit his bands, moved with me to Texas, and, in service to his master's degree, he'd left blues, jazz, and bluegrass behind.

As a playful yet pointed fuck-you to the program, Carrick planned to bow the closing classical composition (I've forgotten which one) during his thesis performance while wearing a full-length white rabbit suit, channeling Mozart as a lunatic Easter bunny. I wanted to stay for the spectacle, but I needed to slip from my aisle seat early to meet the delivery guy who was scheduled to bring several aluminum troughs of pulled pork, brioche buns, and coleslaw for the after-party. As I lugged the hot tins of barbecue past the auditorium's closed double doors I couldn't make out any muffled bass notes, but I could hear the audience suddenly roar and clap.

After the reception we walked back to the car through the dark parking lot. Carrick rolled his upright on its tiny endpin wheel over the asphalt while I carried the white bunny suit slung over one shoulder like a hide. Excited from the rush of performing, he grabbed my hand and swung it back and forth through the air as if we were kids charging across a playground. "Let's give things another shot," he said, turning to me. I looked away and shook my head. "I can't," I answered, letting go of his hand.

. . . .

A couple of weeks before we left Texas, Carrick and I had divided up our possessions and taped shut our cardboard boxes: each one labeled with either my name or his and our different destinations. We then flew to our separate hometowns to visit our families for Thanksgiving. During this time Carrick learned from a mutual friend about the affair I'd had two months earlier that had catalyzed my motivation for the breakup. The friend had e-mailed me an ugly, judgmental diatribe. I instinctively knew from the gratuitous details—dates, locations, hotels—that he'd blind-copied Carrick. He called me immediately. Like the gleeful "Wheeee!" he'd once squalled from the station wagon as it spun over black ice, he opened that final phone call by announcing, theatrically, "Happy Thanksgiving!" I let out a surprised laugh before I sighed. I realized I'd just heard the last joke Carrick would ever tell me. The rest of that conversation remains a stunned, adrenal haze. Did I make excuses? Stutter apologies? I think I asked if he would call me again and he said he didn't know, his voice fraught and exhausted. "I don't want to hear this!" he finally cried, interrupting me, and abruptly hung up.

He soon moved back to Virginia and I took a teaching job in California. He took all of the instruments and I packed the ceramic pots. I noticed Carrick had left behind our stemless wineglasses and wondered if it was because their rims carried the faint coral prints of my lower lip. I slipped an acquaintance our three-foot avocado—the one I'd grown from a toothpicked seed and defended from fruit flies with an invisible troop of mail-ordered nematodes. Since that cold, late November, each time I encounter an upright bass, one body conjures the other—an obvious metonymy. For the first couple of years after the breakup I felt downright implicated in the presence of a string bass. At shows, while the other musicians took turns soloing on piano or mandolin or sax, I'd be gazing the other way, locked in a private spat with the apparition of my missing bassist. Each note seemed to thump out a jazzier version of Poe's pulsing "Tell-Tale Heart." *You're an asshole*, a slapped G would sing at me. *You cheated and you lied*, went the melody. Even if a bass player was clean-shaven and tall and looked nothing at all like Carrick, I'd see my former boyfriend in the way the other musician braced his thumb against the fingerboard or tipped the instrument against his left hip. But the reaction I know would amuse Carrick the most for its screwball panache is this one: whenever I'd see TV cowboys swagger across the screen in old Westerns, their dusty gun holsters reminded me of the quiver-style leather bow holder Carrick would tie to his own thigh at bluegrass shows so he could reach down and slide the stick from the pouch without losing time.

. . . .

What do I do with all of my lost time? With the relationship that took up most of my twenties the way one of Carrick's basses filled a whole corner of our kitchen? We were together for seven years and we haven't spoken once since the awful phone call. Now it seems to me that my twenties were as disproportionate and hulking and lovely as Carrick's upright bass, when he'd fit his endpin wheel into the bottom of the instrument so he could roll the whole thing down the sidewalk. The wheeled bass looked like a sumo wrestler wavering on a unicycle or one of Remedios Varo's surrealist paintings of people with wheels instead of legs. Who knew some relationships are like this—a string bass rolling, elephantine on a single wheel, until a person lets go of the shoulders, releases the neck, lets the body drop?

. . . .

One of our favorite winter walks in Richmond was the three-mile loop from our house on South Cherry through the branching streets of the Fan district (which unfolds on a map in the shape of an antique silk fan) to Video Fan on Strawberry. After choosing a movie we'd swing by Strawberry Street Market to pick up dinner, where Carrick had a shtick going with the funny gay clerk who served fried chicken and vinegar-soaked greens at the deli counter. They'd developed a good-natured butch/femme routine in which they each played to their own stereotype: Carrick's burly mountain redneck to the clerk's effeminate preening queen. Carrick would demand to know the clerk's secret collards recipe, shaking his fist like a cartoon villain, and the clerk would sniff, toss his head as he reached for the greens with his metal tongs, and coyly refuse to give up the ingredients. At first the shtick embarrassed me, but I soon learned I could either stand there looking foolish or laugh.

. . . .

I don't believe in ghosts, though I'm easily spooked. I don't know if the orthodontist's office in the old Victorian was haunted. I do know that the upright bass kept implicating me with its fraught embodiment of Carrick and the way it continued to play my former relationship's most painful notes. I'm not sure when I began to hear welcoming melodies rather than caustic ones vibrate from an upright's *f*-holes, or when I started to recognize in the instrument not an enemy but the shape of an old friend. Now when I hear the walking bass line twang during "Dark Hollow" I recall that winding hike Carrick and I took up to Blackwater Falls: the cool shadows scattered from the oak canopy, the toffee-colored tannic water crashing over rock. The bluegrass standard "Little Maggie" brings back the dancing kids flat-footing to a wild tenor banjo solo at the Purple Fiddle and the rich taste of that sandwich on rye I'd order before gigs: grilled provolone, cheddar, cream cheese, and tomato with balsamic. I imagine I won't ever encounter a band's cover of "Who Flung Poo" at a random show, though sometimes I hear that repeating "Wheeee!" trill from a sudden incongruity—something bizarre or weird a student says that seems unintentionally funny. And sometimes I think of Carrick's final farewell, which used to jolt my gut with a smoldering guilt but now comforts me: that handwritten note he'd tucked into a box I'd packed after our Thanksgiving phone call. *It doesn't matter what you did or how big you fucked up*, he wrote. *Everyone deserves kindness. Life is worth living. You have work to do.*

MODIFYING THE BADGER

Transforming a badger into a raccoon demands a Dremel tool and at least two types of saws. For my second class at Prey Taxidermy—the studio in downtown Los Angeles run by the taxidermist and former Disney employee Allis Markham—I'd signed up for the Sunday workshop called Mammal Shoulder Mounts. Because my creature's hide belonged to an older male raccoon—a boar—I needed to modify a cast polyurethane badger form to fit the skin, since a standard raccoon form would be too small for my imposing specimen. The goal of the course was to "focus on the intricacies of mammal faces" and involved the arrangement of skinned and tanned hides over commercial taxidermy forms to create busts known as "shoulder mounts." I'd chosen a raccoon instead of a coyote since the grizzled canines reminded me of underfed German shepherds. I admired a previously mounted raccoon hanging on the wall near the studio's sink for its subversive whimsy: it was as if someone considered the scrappy mammal a noble trophy, a hunter's graceful whitetail stag. Instead, the animal, peering down from a wooden wall plaque through its black bandit's mask, challenged viewers to contemplate the artfulness of California roadkill or the charm of garbage can invaders exterminated by Salt Lake City's Animal Services.

Tim Bovard, the head taxidermist at the Natural History Museum of Los Angeles County, was guest teaching the mammal course at Allis's studio. He asked the eight students to draw numbers from a bowl so we could take turns picking our hides. (Upon registration online, we'd been asked to check a box marked "Coyote" or "Raccoon" to reserve our preferred species.) Similarly to my first taxidermy course at Prey, a weekend workshop called Birds 101, in which only one of ten students was male, the participants in Mammal Shoulder Mounts were all women: an amateur boxer in her twenties who specialized in anthropomorphic mice, a middle-aged hippie with a brass peace sign belt buckle, a mother and daughter duo from Montana, a blue-haired thirty-something, a wisecracking Southerner, a quiet San Francisco barista, and a woman with tattooed arms and what appeared to be collagen-injected lips and huge silicone boobs at which I kept accidentally staring (she'd gotten the only available bobcat). Tim passed a bowl around the room, and I drew a folded slip of paper marked with the number one, which meant I got first dibs on the raccoon hides. The pelts resembled a stash of hand puppets from someone's nightmare: eyeless raccoons and coyotes with scabrous lids, slack mouths, and lips like the jagged hems of gnawed-on leather gloves. Because Tim had mentioned that the person who chose the large boar raccoon would need to modify a badger form to fit the skin, I immediately seized the hole-filled hide, its yellowed fur streaked with white. I liked the idea of my animal being a shapeshifter.

· · · · · · · · · · · ·

A few months ago, my former poetry mentor Lee visited my husband David and me in Venice, California. We'd invited him to give a reading at our university in celebration of his new book. After Lee finished his last poem and the audience clapped, students began raising their hands. One woman asked Lee's advice for people who have difficultly writing about themselves. "That's a rare problem!" Lee joked from the podium, removing his teal-rimmed reading glasses and then pushing them back up his nose. "There is no one self," he continued, now serious. "We're always inventing ourselves in poems, so to write about the self is to write about multiple selves. The self is malleable."

For years Lee dissuaded me from writing autobiographically. He encouraged me to model my work after that of his favorite contemporary poet, Norman Dubie, a writer who often assumes the voices of historical figures or invented characters in the form of the dramatic monologue. Dubie might speak through the mask of an escaped slave, a young woman in a leper colony, or an insomniac racecar driver. The reason Lee asks young poets to write persona poems, he explained to the attendees, is that "stepping into other people's skins allows them to realize that when they write about themselves it's actually a created personality." "Your own self," he added, "is one of many selves. We're not always the same person."

. . . .

The adjective *personal*, from the Latin *personalis* ("of a person"), has a number of meanings. According to the *Oxford English Dictionary*, these include: "belonging to a particular person rather than to anyone else"; "of or concerning one's private life, relationships, and emotions rather than one's public or professional career"; "relating to a person's body"; and "existing as a self-aware entity, not as an abstraction or an impersonal force."

In C. D. Wright's poem "Personals," the author creates, through juxtaposition, an assemblage of luminous details that compose a self—multivalent and fragmentary. Wright also slyly subverts the conventions of the genre of the personal ad—its generalizations and idealizations—with her assortment of singular desires, charming idiosyncrasies, strange memories, and intimate confessions. Instead of claiming to like movies or long walks on the beach, Wright's candid, deadpan speaker announces, as if in the context of a newspaper's oddest personals column:

> Some nights I sleep with my dress on. My teeth
> are small and even. I don't get headaches.
> Since 1971 or before, I have hunted a bench
> where I could eat my pimento cheese in peace.
> If this were Tennessee and across that river, Arkansas,
> I'd meet you in West Memphis tonight. We could
> have a big time. Danger, shoulder soft.
> Do not lie or lean on me. I'm still trying to find a job
> for which a simple machine isn't better suited.
> I've seen people die of money. Look at Admiral Benbow. I wish
> like certain fishes, we came equipped with light organs.
> Which reminds me of a little-known fact:
> if we were going the speed of light, this dome
> would be shrinking while we were gaining weight.
> Isn't the road crooked and steep.
> In this humidity, I make repairs by night. I'm not one
> among millions who saw Monroe's face
> in the moon. I go blank looking at that face.
> If I could afford it I'd live in hotels. I won awards
> in spelling and the Australian crawl. Long long ago.
> Grandmother married a man named Ivan. The men called him
> Eve. Stranger, to tell the truth, in dog years I am up there.

Through accumulation and refraction, Wright's slivers of personal history in "Personals" expand into a larger social matrix, a collection of artifacts linked to the speaker of the poem, but also to the history and cultural heritage of the United Kingdom and the United States: the tragic figures of Admiral Benbow of the Royal Navy and Marilyn Monroe, the shapeshifting craters of the moon's face, ominous echoes of an anthropomorphic road sign ("Danger, shoulder soft"), and Bill Withers's lyrics, warped and eerie ("Do not lie or lean on me"). Wright's last line directly addresses the anonymous reader of the personal ad (as well as the reader of the poem) through a witty evasion: "Stranger, to tell the truth, in dog years I am up there." In "Personals," Wright implies that what makes up a self, body, private life, or personal force is that unique mixture of pathos and humor, revelation and concealment, banality and wonder. She transforms the impersonal character of a simple "lonely hearts" ad into the complex and intimate helix of a deeply layered self.

. . . .

Madison Rubin, Tim's apprentice at the Natural History Museum, a woman who grew up in LA's Brewery Art Colony, told me that she'd modified several taxidermy forms to suit the skins of incongruous creatures. She'd made a llama and an alpaca, each out of a deer form, by elongating the ruminants' necks. And she'd radically reduced the scale of a fawn form to make a white-eyed baby goat for a Satanic altar.

Before his thirty-year museum career, Tim had worked for a time as a commercial taxidermist, creating trophy mounts for hunters. He warned us that the worst thing a person could do to fishermen's catch was to mount and return the fish at exactly the same size—he regularly enlarged specimens to buoy the hunters' pride.

But even with enlargement, it's better to have a slightly smaller form to work with, Tim noted, since looser skin is easier to move around than a tightly fitting hide.

The tanned hides of my classmates' coyotes smelled like wet dogs and dill pickles. I was surprised that my raccoon skin didn't give off much of a scent—just the slightest musk of truffle oil or dusty attic. The jumble of polyurethane taxidermy forms the color of old elephant tusks sat on top of the industrial fridge. They had a waxy patina and looked like a herd of phantom animals of indeterminate species, partial-bodied and born without ears or eyes. The angular coyote forms resembled the blond ghosts of greyhounds, and the chubby raccoons recalled small albino seals. In order to turn my fat badger form into that of a slightly slimmer boar raccoon, I needed to slice off the sides of its broad, wedge-shaped skull with a circular saw, shorten the snout with a handsaw, narrow the jowls with a metal file, carve out new eye sockets and define the lip line with a Dremel tool, and sand down the rough edges to give the remade face "flow."

In order to sculpt realistic expressions while taxidermying our mammals—alertness, curiosity, sleepiness, fear—we needed to scratch the smooth surfaces of the animal forms with a wire brush before gluing down our skins. This way, Tim said, the sticky, purple hide paste (which looked like buttercream icing dyed mauve and smelled like vanilla) would bind more securely to the polyurethane. And a firm bond better enables the skin to "hold the detail" as the taxidermist shapes it around simulated muscles—the bulge of a cheek or upward jut of a chin—making the face expressive, supple, and seemingly alive.

Avoid giving your animal a smile, Tim advised, as we began doing a "skin tuck" with our lip tools, jamming the rough and scabby mouth edges into the carved ditch of the lip line. As the hide dries, Tim warned us, a smile will often shift into a grimace.

· · · · · · · · · · · ·

Recently I taught Jack Gilbert's poem "Trying to Have Something Left Over" to a group of creative writing students in my introductory-level poetry course. In the poem, Gilbert evokes the end of an affair between a married American speaker and his Danish lover, who has a young son:

> There was a great tenderness to the sadness
> when I would go there. She knew how much
> I loved my wife and that we had no future.
> We were like casualties helping each other
> as we waited for the end. Now I wonder
> if we understood how happy those Danish
> afternoons were. Most of the time we did not talk.
> Often I took care of the baby while she did
> housework. Changing him and making him laugh.
> I would say *Pittsburgh* softly each time before
> throwing him up. Whisper *Pittsburgh* with
> my mouth against the tiny ear and throw
> him higher. Pittsburgh and happiness high up.
> The only way to leave even the smallest trace.
> So that all his life her son would feel gladness
> unaccountably when anyone spoke of the ruined
> city of steel in America. Each time almost
> remembering something maybe important that got lost.

As I launched into my spiel about how Gilbert's poem explores a nuanced, ambivalent, and very grown-up perception of love (its ebbs and flows, its contradictions and betrayals), I noticed several students making skeptical faces. "It's both compassionate and complicated,"

I continued, referring to Gilbert's vision of the tender yet doomed affair. A contingent of the class couldn't believe that the speaker would cheat on his wife if he loved her. The wife had to be dead, one woman argued. He wouldn't have had an affair. No way. I glanced around the room to see other students nodding. Gently, I pointed out that several other poems in Gilbert's collection reinforce the circumstance of the affair, including the poem "Infidelity," in which a man promises his wife he'll end his affair with a married woman who has a child. "The speaker's affair with the Danish woman doesn't necessarily mean he no longer loves his wife," I suggested. "Sometimes we become different versions of ourselves, different people, depending on the company." Surprisingly, within the sadness of this fraught time, Gilbert's speaker makes a final gesture toward happiness as he whispers, "Pittsburgh," like a shibboleth, into the ear of his lover's baby. "So that all his life her son would feel gladness / unaccountably when anyone spoke of the ruined / city of steel in America," Gilbert writes, imagining strange waves of joyous déjà vu for the child, a lifelong Pavlovian response: "Each time almost / remembering something maybe important that got lost."

. . . .

Tim told me the story of his piecemeal polar bear as I tucked the edges of my raccoon's eyelids to form a clean border between the skin and glass eyes. Tim had needed a polar bear for the new exhibit he was to create for the Natural History Museum, which was scheduled to open in two years. He'd submitted requests to several zoos around the country for a specimen (if a captive polar bear died, he'd receive the corpse), but he couldn't secure one in time. After digging around the museum's storage facility, however, he managed to find several old polar bear rugs from the 1960s and decided to create from the multiple furs a single, composite animal. Because the hides had been acid tanned, making the skins tight and inflexible, and due to their blunt, square "rug" shapes, he and Madison cut the furs into hundreds of intricate pieces, arranged them over a handmade bear form they'd constructed, and glued down the mosaicked hide. No one could tell the museum's new polar bear was an improvised patchwork.

As I banged out the rounded triangular shapes I'd cut from sheet lead with a hammer and anvil to make the inner scaffolding for my raccoon's ears, Tim told me a story he referred to as the "live pig tattoo." During the sixties Tim knew a pot-smoking pig farmer, who, as a joke, tattooed wings on the back of one of his own prize hogs, in honor of the cliché, "When pigs fly." The figure of speech is considered an adynaton, a type of hyperbole so exaggerated and ridiculous that it shifts into an impossibility.

Rilke conjures the impossible unicorn—"the creature that doesn't exist"—in his fourth poem in the second series of *The Sonnets to Orpheus*, translated by A. Poulin, Jr. The unicorn can become a living animal, Rilke suggests, if people love it, if their imaginations are bold enough, if they nourish the mythical beast with the power of their belief. "They didn't feed it with corn," Rilke writes, "but always with the chance that it might / be."

. . . .

While raccoons have a reputation for ferocity and brashness, I've learned that they're also surprisingly delicate: they can hear earthworms shimmy beneath the soil and their paw skin prickles and becomes more sensitive when slick with rain. The reason for raccoons' distinctive black "masks" on their salt-and-pepper coats may be an evolutionary improvement meant to reduce glare and boost night vision, making it easier for the mammals to locate foes in the dark. Most raccoons, whose scientific name *lotor* means, in

Latin, "the washer," instinctively dip their food in water before eating it. The meanest trick you can play on a raccoon, a friend and science writer once told me, is to give it a sugar cube. The creature will eagerly scurry to a river or creek to rinse the treat, only to find, as it raises its fingers to its face, that the sugar cube has dissolved, leaving its paws empty.

. . . .

To my dismay, my raccoon's softly alert expression had dried into a droopy, demented snarl. His snout sagged and one of his eyelids peeled back, giving him a rabid, snaggletoothed countenance. He looked like the demonic villain in some sort of dark, adult puppet theater or a piece of resurrected roadkill in a bad horror movie. Madison helped me pry the glued-on hide from the modified badger form so I could re-create some of the missing flesh beneath the animal's muzzle and under the eyelids by sticking coils of clay to the polyurethane. Once the skin was re-secured, Tim bent over to scrutinize my raccoon's newly supple expression. "The Old Boar," he said, nodding. Because boar raccoons are so vicious and prone to fights, he told me, their hides are often scarred from scuffles, and sometimes they even bite off one another's tails: "They look like they've been through the wars."

A few weeks later I returned to Prey for additional finishing work on my shoulder mount. My raccoon still wore an old wound in the middle of his forehead—a golf ball–sized patch of bald skin between his eyes. After I shampooed and conditioned his coarse fur in the studio's sink (I felt like a hairdresser in a salon for discerning wildlife), I removed the bald patch of hide on his forehead with an X-Acto blade, leaving a clean, diamond-shaped hole. I cut a matching scrap from a different raccoon hide—another grizzled old boar streaked with yellow and white—and patched the hole by gluing down the piece of new hide with epoxy. I painted my raccoon's dried nose and clay "tear ducts" with black acrylic, adding a layer of clear gloss to make the nose appear moist and placing a single drop of gloss at the edge of his lips to mimic a spot of saliva. I combed the bristles of the old and new hides together, blending the borders of the patch to disguise the seams, and added streaks of white and black paint to align the mismatched patterns.

. . . .

"Why taxidermy?" a friend of mine asked me during a dinner out. I was visiting her university to give a poetry reading. "Anna," she said, leaning over the white tablecloth while clutching her glass of Chardonnay, "isn't taxidermy for creepy dudes who still live in their mothers' basements?" I laughed and told her she had a point, then described the young women who worked at Prey like Allis and Madison, how our specimens were "ethically sourced," and how I thought the bodies of animals were beautiful. My friend looked unconvinced.

I've asked myself the same question. Why taxidermy? I've taken two classes: an avian workshop and a mammal course. I've taxidermied a European starling and a scrappy Utah raccoon, but I don't plan on continuing in the craft. I won't be taxidermying my cat Jellybean when she goes or my friend's aging Chihuahua. Bringing a dead animal back to "life" through taxidermy—by shaping confident details and lines, by conjuring a fantastic world in which this impossible form might exist—is similar to writing a poem, I think, and, significantly, both modes of art are acutely linked to loss. The lyric moment, frozen in an arrangement of raccoon hide or bird skin or within the precise imagery and syntax of a poem, creates an illusion for the viewer or reader that moves beyond reality: we're offered a moment that testifies to the beauty, bittersweetness, and gravity of impermanence, and yet, paradoxically, that moment and its inhabitants are no longer mortal. They stand with the other shapeshifters, defiant, outside of time. Like Tim's piecemeal polar bear, my patched boar raccoon, or Rilke's summoned unicorn, the lyric moment becomes immortal. Who wouldn't want to reach out and capture that?

BLUEBEARD'S CLOSET

I visited the Museum of Death to see the preserved head of Henri Désiré Landru, the serial killer known as "the Bluebeard of Paris." In 1922 Landru was guillotined for murdering ten of his fiancées, as well as one woman's teenage son. Although no bodies were ever recovered, the prosecuting attorney argued that Landru dismembered his victims and incinerated their body parts in his coal-fired stove. The vanished women, most of them war widows, had responded to the fraudulent personal ads Landru had placed in Parisian newspapers, in which he'd posed as a wealthy widower. Beneath the Museum of Death's glass display dome, Landru's gaunt face recalled the color and texture of charcoal, and his fibrous lips looked like the edges of a dried mango slice. The murderer's facial hair—a black Van Dyke beard and waxed mustache—had been shaved in preparation for the guillotine. As my husband inspected the adjacent exhibit (a full-size replica of Florida's electric chair), I stood to one side of Landru's mummified head so other visitors could lean in.

The museum, founded in 1995, with branches in Los Angeles and New Orleans, aims to "fill the void of death education in the USA." Certain exhibits I avoided entirely. Others I encountered by accident (like John Wayne Gacy's eerie paintings of Pogo the Clown) and hurried past. The California Death Room—which I glimpsed from the hallway but refused to enter—offered a gruesome wallpaper: an ensemble of crime scene photographs from the Charles Manson murders. I turned down one corridor decorated with enlarged color photographs of American soldiers sprawled on battlefields in Iraq and Afghanistan, then pivoted toward another hall. As I turned to the broad left wall, I realized I stood nose level with a spread of black-and-white photographs of 1950s automobile accidents, with decapitated or maimed bodies slumped over seats and steering wheels. I looked away, hoping no one had noticed, and escaped to a side room.

Other exhibits at the Museum of Death captivated me. I lingered over the collection of logo-engraved pocketknives from 1970s funeral homes. I admired the tender mementos of Victorian mourning jewelry: the silver pins and lockets that held intimate wisps of a dead beloved's now mouse-colored hair. I paused in front of a case of formidable prison shivs from Alabama. My favorite display was the small room packed to its ceiling with taxidermy. In the hallway entrance to the room sat two celebrity-owned pets: Liberace's grizzled blond cat, Candy, and an apprehensive-looking Chihuahua that had expired alongside Jayne Mansfield in the actress's 1967 car accident. Inside the room, I squatted to examine the contents of a lower shelf: a black-humored barbecue tool-set in which the legs of deer formed the trophy handles of the grilling utensils—fork, brush, knife, spatula, two skewers—each one tipped in a hoof.

I spent the longest amount of time standing in front of an entire wall of albino animals: a white muskrat, squirrel, possum, skunk, fox, fawn, and nearly impossible to recognize flaxen raccoon striped in faint amber. What are the chances that this uniquely phosphorescent herd might meet and decide to travel together through a forest? The only suitable vista in which they could survive and seek camouflage would be an arctic one: pure white. The animals—red-eyed, platinum-bristled—crouched in a Siberian pastoral, that winter fable that never got told, or translated, in time.

. . . .

In 1964 my mother joined a social club during her freshman year at Mississippi State College for Women, in Columbus, and as part of her pledge duties, the Lancers asked her to tell a story to the group. She picked "Bluebeard" and performed the tale in a brooding, theatrical voice. Her selection of a story in which a deranged serial killer slaughters multiple women and tosses them into a secret chamber may seem at first a perverse choice for an audience of students who attended a small women's college in the Deep South. But the horror story must've had a special resonance among women at the cusp of looking toward their future lives, many of them as young wives. In 1964, only a year since the publication of Betty Friedan's *The Feminine Mystique,* the students at Mississippi State College for Women had to reckon with the lingering conventions of 1950s domesticity (as well as the particular regional tradition of the Southern belle) and the beginnings of the second-wave feminist movement. My mother wore embroidered peasant blouses, grew out her hair, and sang in a folk trio, the Guineveres, but she also practiced walking with a book balanced on top of her head during her required college course Personal Appearance. In the class, the male teacher would inspect his students' nude pantyhose and subtract a point for each white run. The women had a midnight dorm curfew on the weekends, with a male dean in charge of its enforcement. On weekdays, men were forbidden on campus. What must "Bluebeard" have said, in this context, about sexual power dynamics? What must it have meant to my mother?

. . . .

Multiple versions of the "Bluebeard" story exist. Since Charles Perrault's original tale, writers and artists as various as the Brothers Grimm, Béla Bartók, Sylvia Plath, and Margaret Atwood have added their visions to that enduring horror story of sexual politics. Nothing supernatural happens in Perrault's version—unless you count the key's indelible bloodstain as supernaturally obstinate— thus "Bluebeard" is technically a cautionary tale rather than a fairy tale. Perrault, the seventeenth-century French author, published his influential *Stories or Tales of Past Times with Morals* (subtitled *Tales of Mother Goose*), in 1697, when he was nearly seventy. The slim yet celebrated book includes only eight tales. My copy of his "*La Barbe Bleue*," which bears the Americanized title "The Whimsical History of Bluebeard," first belonged to my maternal grandparents. The oversized yellow volume is part of their handsome collector's set titled *The Evergreen Tales; or Tales for the Ageless* (1952), translated by the British writer and critic Arthur Quiller-Couch and illustrated by the Danish painter Hans Bendix. My grandfather subscribed to the Limited Editions Club, based in New York, and filled the shelves of his home library with rare, leather-bound books in shades of ruby, topaz, sandalwood, and plum. I especially loved the sinister wood-block prints in Dante's *Divine Comedy* and the special edition of Jonathan Swift's *Gulliver's Travels*. The two volumes of Swift's work came with their own upholstered carrying case that had a vast slot for the cutting-board–sized hardcover *A Voyage to Brobdingnag* and a narrow groove for the miniature volume *A Voyage to Lilliput*. My grandfather's limited edition of "Bluebeard" is number 1052, out of two thousand copies, and the general editor, Jean Hersholt, signed its final page in faint lapis ink. As a child, I used to touch the embossed spines of my grandparents' books, believing their gilt titles were inlaid with real gold. As a child, my mother sat on the red Turkish rug in her parents' library and turned the pages of the story, fascinated by Bendix's gestural watercolors, particularly his illustration of the villain's forbidden room.

In Perrault's "Bluebeard," a repulsively ugly widower, who lives in a castle and belongs to the vulgar *nouveau riche*, marries the young aristocratic woman Fatima, who resolves to overlook her suitor's hideous blue beard. Before leaving town on business, Bluebeard gives his new bride the keys to the castle, including one that unlocks the door of the chamber he's forbidden her to enter. Predictably, Fatima can't suppress her curiosity and unlocks the door to reveal the corpses of Bluebeard's former wives. In her horror she drops the key, staining the metal with blood. Bluebeard returns early, discovers the bloody key, then threatens to decapitate Fatima. She begs for a few minutes to say her prayers, which gives her time to enlist her older sister Anne's help. Anne stands on the roof and waves a kerchief as a distress signal to their brothers, who approach the castle on horseback. The brothers speed up as they notice Anne, burst through the castle doors, and stab Bluebeard to death with their swords, rescuing Fatima.

As baffling as Perrault's cautionary tale may be (what drives Bluebeard's perverse demands and reactionary violence?), it remains one of the most widely known stories in the folk tale canon. Bluebeard refuses to explain or repent his violence; we never understand what mysterious circumstances drive him toward serial murder. In his classic Freudian exploration of the meaning and significance of fairy tales *The Uses of Enchantment* (1976), the Austrian-born American psychologist Bruno Bettelheim argues that "Bluebeard" advocates

a "humane morality which understands and forgives sexual trans-
gressions." "Marital infidelity," Bettelheim suggests, "symbolically
expressed by the blood . . . on the key, is something to be forgiven."

But "[i]s this tale truly about marital discord?" asks Jack Zipes
in *Why Fairy Tales Stick* (2006). Neither partner marries for love,
Zipes notes. Bluebeard weds for status and Fatima for money.
Fatima profits from Bluebeard's death, remarries, and forgets her
past. Bluebeard remains opaque and unknowable. We discover
alongside Fatima his murderous secret but we never understand his
reasoning or intents. He veers from laughing amiably at a prank
(Fatima and her sister chop off the stem of Bluebeard's rare aloe that
blooms only once per century) to brutally attempting to decapitate
his bride. Zipes doesn't believe readers seek out "Bluebeard" for the
wise insights into marriage it provides; he thinks we're drawn to
the story for its puzzling, provocative explorations of "the instinc-
tual drive for power that misfires." I suspect my mother didn't tell
"Bluebeard" to the Southern belles pledging the Lancers to help
them become more obedient wives. I suspect she told the Lancers—those women named after lance-wielding soldiers—as an act
of celebratory defiance. Who hasn't wanted to pry open a secret?

"We open the successive doors in Bluebeard's castle because
'they are there,'" writes cultural critic George Steiner in his treatise
on the decline of classical humanism *In Bluebeard's Castle* (1971).
"[E]ach leads to the next," he continues:

> by a logic of intensification which is that of the mind's
> own awareness of being. To leave one door closed
> would be not only cowardice but a betrayal—radical,
> self-mutilating—of the inquisitive, probing, forward-
> tensed stance of our species. We are hunters after real-
> ity, wherever it may lead.

. . . .

To find out whether she wanted to become a psychiatrist, like her father, my mother worked in Seven East, the psychiatric wing of the University of Mississippi Medical Center, during the summer between her freshman and sophomore years of college. My grandfather, Dr. L. C. Hanes, taught and practiced psychiatry in Jackson from 1959 until his death in 1987. He worked at the Medical Center during a number of those years. My mother's main duties as a psychiatric aide involved socializing with the patients in Seven East—chatting with them and playing bridge. One of the patients, my mother learned, was on suicide watch and required special protocol. My mother was supposed to "01 her," which meant she was to carefully shadow the patient, whom I'll call Ruth. Ruth was in her early twenties, shorthaired, slight, and wiry. Her father had often left her alone as a child with her depressed mother while he went away on business, and, during one trip, Ruth's mother killed herself. Until her own suicide attempt during her first year of college, Ruth had been a student at Millsaps College. She had an IQ of 160 and a scornful nickname for my mother—"Turd"—a word that wasn't yet part of my sheltered mother's vocabulary. One day, my mother peered into Ruth's room through the door's small observational window, but the space looked empty. As soon as my mother opened the door and stepped inside, Ruth quickly slipped out of the room, slamming the door behind her, which locked automatically. Although my mother wasn't stuck in the "01" room for long and staff members soon located Ruth in another part of the hospital, my mom decided not to pursue a career in psychiatry. Ruth finally learned upon her return that Dr. Hanes was my mother's father. "You're Father *Hanes's* daughter," Ruth said reverentially, figuring my grandfather as a priest, her confessor. From then on, she called my mother "Father Hanes's Daughter" instead of "Turd."

. . . .

The expression "skeleton in the closet" arose in the early nineteenth century. In an article published in the UK monthly periodical the *Eclectic Review*, the minister and editor William Hendry Stowell employs the metaphor as a description of the urge to keep hidden from family members the knowledge of hereditary diseases. "The dread of being the cause of misery to posterity," Stowell writes, "has prevailed over men to conceal the skeleton in the closet." The *Oxford English Dictionary* offers the following definitions of the expression: "a private and concealed trouble in one's house or circumstances, ever present, and ever liable to come into view" and "a secret source of shame or pain to a family or person." The phrase's exact origins remain mysterious. Although Perrault's chamber of corpses in "Bluebeard" suggests one plausible source, a number of people have surmised that the image of the hidden skeleton refers to the clandestine use of anatomy skeletons by physicians or artists who had not received legal permission to dissect corpses. Thus, people interested in directly exploring the human body—or academics who wished to use cadavers as teaching tools—kept their black-market materials discreetly tucked away, locked in wardrobes, cupboards, or closets.

For years, my grandfather kept a secret in his closet.

. . . .

My grandfather saved a fragment of the skull of his medical school skeleton. Throughout his studies at UT Austin, he'd used the yellow, bowl-shaped hunk of parietal bone as an ashtray, finally deciding that doing so was in poor taste and retiring the object to a cardboard box in the attic. Most of the patients he treated at the University of Mississippi Medical Center were female neurotics or gay adolescent males. Although my grandfather never shared privileged information about patients with his family, my mother suspected that he urged his gay patients to accept themselves rather than seek some dubious "cure" for their sexuality. He actively steered the teenagers away from a particular colleague of his at the Medical Center who specialized in an insidious form of "behavior modification therapy" for gay men, which involved attaching electrodes to the patients' testicles, projecting slides of nude men and women on a screen, and shocking the patients' genitals each time a picture of a naked man materialized. "He got apoplectic about that doctor," my mom said. Throughout his career, my grandfather remained skeptical about treatments that aimed to change a person's fundamental character, including electroconvulsive therapy. His own mother, depressed since her oldest daughter Joyce died from strep throat, suffered severe brain damage from early electroshock treatments. Before the final round of shock therapy launched her into a permanent vegetative state, she experienced a psychotic break and chased my grandfather's other sister, seven-year-old Jeannette, into the backyard waving a BB gun. Jeanette shimmied up a chinaberry as her mother fired at her, pacing back and forth in the grass below. The little girl stayed in the tree until her father returned from the barbershop to steer his wife back inside.

. . . .

Although I'm attached to my grandparents' copy of Perrault's "Bluebeard," I prefer the early nineteenth-century version of the story retold by the Brothers Grimm, titled "Fitcher's Bird." The Grimms' revision of "Bluebeard" remains similar in plot to Perrault's, although it contains a number of supernatural elements, which makes their story a true fairy tale rather than a cautionary one. In "Fitcher's Bird," the Bluebeard figure isn't a rich man in a castle; he's a wizard in a dark forest. The wizard dresses up as a beggar, lugging on his back a magical wicker basket into which he compels women to jump. During one outing, he arrives at the home of a family with three daughters, makes the oldest sibling hop into his basket, and carries her to his house in the woods. In addition to giving his kidnapped bride-to-be the key to the forbidden room, he hands her an egg, which she must carry at all times. Like Fatima in "Bluebeard," the oldest sister unlocks the wizard's forbidden room and discovers the bodies of murdered women. The Grimms' macabre vision of the carnage surpasses Perrault's in its violence: the wizard had dismembered his victims and dumped the hacked-up parts into a bloody basin in the center of the chamber. Instead of dropping the key, she lets go of the egg, staining its shell with blood. The wizard returns, slaughters the oldest sister, returns to the family's house, and snatches the middle sister, with whom he repeats the murderous scenario. The youngest sister, however, outsmarts the wizard after she's kidnapped, tucking away the egg for safekeeping before she enters the forbidden room. She notices her sisters' corpses among the bodies, and, horrified, reaches into the bloody basin to recover their severed limbs, arranging them in order, like human puzzle pieces: "head, body, arms and legs." "And when nothing further was lacking," the Brothers Grimm recount, "the limbs began to move and unite themselves together, and both the maidens opened their eyes and were once more alive. Then they rejoiced and kissed and caressed each other."

Unlike Fatima in Perrault's "Bluebeard," who remains passive as she relies on her siblings to devise her rescue, the youngest sister in "Fitcher's Bird" brings about her own salvation. When the wizard returns, he finds the egg pristine. "He now had no longer any power over her," the Brothers Grimm write, "and was forced to do whatsoever she desired." The young woman hides her resurrected sisters in the wizard's basket, covers them with a layer of gold, and forces him to deliver the load to her parents while she pretends to prepare the wedding feast. She invites the wizard's friends. She invents a double for herself: a grinning skull wreathed in flowers, which she places in an upstairs window. Next, "she got into a barrel of honey, and then cut the feather-bed open and rolled herself in it, until she looked like a wondrous bird, and no one could recognize her." She flees the house and slips past wedding guests on their way to the celebration, answering their questions with her savvy birdlike song:

> "O, Fitcher's bird, how com'st thou here?"
> "I come from Fitcher's house quite near."
> "And what may the young bride be doing?"
> "From cellar to garret she's swept all clean,
> And now from the window she's peeping I ween."

She meets the wizard on his way back to the house, fooling him, too. The fairy tale ends when the family of the bride arrives at the feast, locks the wizard and his friends in the house, and burns the place to the ground.

I prefer "Fitcher's Bird" to "Bluebeard" for its unstable, shifting power dynamics and for the central female character's agency and resourcefulness. She doesn't just quiver in terror, hoping Bluebeard won't notice her betrayal. She restores her sisters' bodies to wholeness and transforms herself into a golden bird, making for herself a magical skin from honey and feathers.

. . . .

In his classic phenomenological text *The Poetics of Space* (1958), the French philosopher Gaston Bachelard explores the spaces—cellars, attics, corners, and more—that comprise a home. In the chapter "Drawers, Chests, and Wardrobes," Bachelard describes these "hiding-places in which human beings, great dreamers of locks, keep or hide their secrets." Elsewhere, he writes:

> Wardrobes with their shelves, desks with their drawers, and chests with their false bottoms are veritable organs of the secret psychological life. Indeed, without these "objects" and a few others in equally high favor, our intimate life would lack a model of intimacy. They are hybrid objects, subject objects. Like us, through us and for us, they have a quality of intimacy.

> Does there exist a single dreamer of words who does not respond to the word wardrobe? . . . . .

> And to fine words correspond fine things, to grave-sounding words, an entity of depth. Every poet of furniture—even if he be a poet in a garret, and therefore has no furniture—knows that the inner space of an old wardrobe is deep. A wardrobe's inner space is also *intimate space*, space that is not open to just anybody.

C. S. Lewis famously employed the intimate space of a wardrobe as a fantastical portal into the land of Narnia, filled with marvelous talking animals, mythological creatures, and a fearsome White Witch. Most "poets of furniture," however, evoke more ambivalent and haunting figurations of the secret space. In Bill Knott's poem "The Closet," a young speaker opens his mother's wardrobe (after she had died in childbirth) to find "the hangers arc sharper, knife 'n' slice, I jump / Helplessly to catch them to twist them clear . . . ." In Saeed Jones's "Closet of Red," a baroque cascade of foliage blooms within a space that would contain or control queer desire: "In place of *no*, my leaking mouth spills fox-gloves. / Trumpets of tongued blossoms litter the locked closet."

Once, a tattoo artist who had to break his lease gave me a tour of his apartment. I'd responded to the ad he'd posted online about the rental. As I admired a hardcover art book on his coffee table that featured a collection of Alberto Vargas's vintage illustrations of midcentury pinups, he said he often used Vargas's nude women as templates for "naked lady" designs on clients' biceps. I imagined the women would resurrect, like the sisters in "Fitcher's Bird," each time muscles flexed and twitched the tattoos to life. Before I left, he showed me an armoire that came with the apartment since it was solid walnut and too heavy to move. He said he wanted to show me a secret, and lifted the false bottom of the armoire to reveal a hidden compartment lined in purple velvet. Later, after I had moved in, I peeked into the secret drawer and found that he'd left the Vargas book there for me as a gift. The real gift, though, we both knew, was our sharing the intimacy of a secret.

Once, while cleaning out my grandfather's house after his death, my mother discovered a stash of gay porn magazines hidden in a green canvas backpack in his closet.

. . . .

In addition to being a psychiatrist, my grandfather was an amateur painter, a classical guitar player, a fencer, a civil rights activist, an interfaith community leader, and a collector of newfangled technologies. He was the first person on the block to own a color TV. I grew up staring at a framed oil painting he made that hangs on the wall in my father's home office. It's a still life done in a heavy, impressionist impasto: three oranges in a wooden bowl beside a half-filled water pitcher placed on a white-and-blue plaid tablecloth, one end of the material folded back. The perspective is wrong—unintentionally and confusedly cubist. Due to the table's angle, I shouldn't be able to see the tops of the oranges. But I like that I can see them: their skins splotchy and bright, the white light coming in strong and from all directions.

. . . .

The expression "coming out of the closet" is a mixed metaphor. The phrase blends "coming out," which evokes the celebratory "coming-out party" of a debutante, with "skeleton in the closet," which connotes a shameful, hidden secret. So these sociolinguistic origins warp the metaphor's vehicle as well as torque the tone. "Coming out," before the 1950s, suggested an optimistic entrance into society, whereas "coming out of the closet," after the Stonewall Riots, implied an exit from the oppression of a secret.

Although my grandfather never came out of the closet during his lifetime, choosing to remain in a heteronormative marriage, my mother had suspected her father's hidden identity for several decades. Every now and then, she told me, she'd "catch whiffs" of his secret. "Like what?" I'd asked.

My mother, who belonged to a community theater troupe, developed a crush on a costume designer, Bob, who'd moved from New York to Jackson to work on a local play about the true identity of Shakespeare. (This was the play during which the lead actor— the guy who played Shakespeare—succumbed to his flu and threw up on my mother backstage.) She told her father how talented and funny Bob seemed, that he'd make "a nice marriage partner," and that he was bisexual. When my grandfather advised her against pursuing a relationship with Bob, saying it "wasn't a good thing for a woman to enter into," my mother believed he spoke from his perspective as a shrink. She realized much later that he might have spoken from personal experience. Throughout his married life, my grandfather maintained a circle of openly gay friends and invited them over for dinner with his family. There was Leslie, the male choir director at the Episcopalian church at which my grandfather served as a lay reader. There was the interior designer, Hal. There was Jim, a fellow shrink he'd met at the University Medical Center and with whom he founded Riverside, the first psychiatric hospital in the vicinity of Jackson. (The other hospitals in the area offered only psychiatric wings.) My mother remembers Jim coming over for dinner many times with his younger boyfriend Skip, whom Jim was putting through college. They'd play duplicate bridge with my grandparents. After Skip graduated, he left Jim and eventually married a woman. My grandfather would get drunk and drive over, alone, to Jim's house and stay for hours. My mother believes Jim was her father's long-term partner, though she never asked either of them about it, even after her father's death, even after she found the magazines, even after she saw—at the funeral—Jim's anguished face.

. . . .

Part of me grieves for my grandfather's secret: it must've been a harrowing burden to bear. And part of me shivers with the knowledge that his secret is why I'm alive, why my mother, aunt, and sister were born. Four people. I'm grateful. I'm horrified. Didn't he know, as a shrink, that his sacrifice was destructive? How could he advise his patients to accept themselves when he couldn't show that same generosity toward himself? He wore love beads in the sixties. He worked to advance integration policies in Mississippi. He welcomed the Summer of Love. Why didn't he tell his family?

My grandmother had to have known. Before they moved to Jackson, she'd threatened to leave him in New Orleans, even calling her former nursing supervisor in Austin and arranging to return to her old job. What did he have to promise her? When he couldn't give up Jim, why didn't he at least finally tell my mother? Why didn't he live with his lover and find happiness after my grandmother died?

Before my grandmother died from terminal emphysema in 1985, she and my grandfather used the money they'd received from selling their stake in Riverside Psychiatric Hospital to travel the world. In 1981, they visited Paris and London. They flew to Hong Kong, Singapore, Bangkok, and Nepal. They visited my parents and me in suburban Dhaka. Advised against the trip, my grandmother told her doctor that she'd rather die visiting her baby granddaughter in Bangladesh than live in fear in Jackson. She crammed a folder with a two-inch stack of her photocopied medical records and packed it in her suitcase.

During a tour of the yellow, smoky streets of Old Dhaka clogged with rickshaws and ghastly traffic jams, my grandmother began wheezing. My parents took her back to the house while Susheel, their household staff manager, remained with my grandfather, who said he wanted to continue sightseeing. My grandfather returned after midnight, drunk, with a rambling, incoherent tale about how he and Susheel had gotten lost. My mother wonders whether he'd convinced Susheel to take him to a gay brothel.

. . . .

A number of scholars and biographers have suggested that the nineteenth-century Danish author Hans Christian Andersen created an allegorical self-portrait of his bisexuality in the fairy tale "The Little Mermaid," originally titled "The Daughters of the Air."

As early as 1907, Andersen's biographer Hans Brix equated the Little Mermaid's unrequited love for the prince with Andersen's love for his male friend, Edvard Collin, who married a woman. Andersen wrote love poems to Collin and confessed, in a letter: "How I long for you, Edvard! I think the separation has turned my friendship into love." Andrew Teverson suggests in *Fairy Tale* (2013) that "Andersen is the suffering half-half creature, unable to speak his love, but also unable to give it up." Like the hybrid mermaid, who must choose between sea and land, body and spirit, Andersen must negotiate opposing geographic and existential realms: between the Odense of his childhood and the Copenhagen of his adult life, between erotic and literary fulfillment. Andersen, like his mermaid, strives to win the love of a man who can't return his affections. According to Jackie Wullschlager's biography, *Hans Christian Andersen: The Life of a Storyteller* (2000), Andersen couldn't accept that the mermaid's acquisition of an immortal soul depended on the reciprocal love of a man. He couldn't bear to let her die and turn into nothingness—a layer of empty, golden foam floating on the surface of the sea. He revised his story so that even though the Little Mermaid doesn't find happiness with her prince, she becomes one of the rare ethereal sprites called the "daughters of the air" who fly around doing good deeds for hundreds of years, eventually creating their own immortal souls. Wullschlager suggests that Andersen substituted his erotic desires with his literary ambition and longing for fame. Toward the end of his life, she notes, Andersen wrote to congratulate a young correspondent on his recent marriage, saying:

> "You have got yourself a home, a loving wife, and
> you are happy! God bless you and her! At one time
> I too dreamed of such happiness, but it was not to

be granted to me. Happiness came to me in another form, came as my muse that gave me a wealth of adventure and songs."

What must've Andersen felt when Edvard Collin married Henriette Thyberg? He wrote to his friend: "My dear, dear Edvard—God bless and go with you!" He then evoked, in harrowing detail, the Little Mermaid's anguish: every step she took on her new legs felt like "walking on knives." Finally, Andersen rested beside his friend in death, when Collin granted the author's wish: Collin, his wife, and Andersen were interred side by side, as a threesome. Years later, the bodies of the married couple were exhumed by relatives and buried in a family plot, leaving Andersen alone in the grave.

. . . .

"Never get sick on a Saturday," my grandfather liked to say, "or a Sunday." Holidays were out, too. Why, then, did he schedule his hernia operation for a weekend, when the regular full-time staff would be gone? He must've considered the surgery too routine to worry about. He didn't know that the doctor would knick an artery; that the cavity of his chest would slowly fill with blood overnight; that by the time he rose in the dark, thinking the pressure in his gut meant he had to pee, he realized he was bleeding out. As he fell to the floor of his hospital bathroom he yanked the emergency lever.

My grandfather died from the botched hernia operation when he was sixty-two, at least twenty years before he should have. He died when I was seven, when I was too young to know him. He should have lived into his eighties, like everyone else's grandparents, Skyping with me from my dorm room and politely complimenting my maudlin early poems. He should have lived to see popular opinion about gay rights—and civil rights laws—change. I don't know if the memories I have of him are actual ones or whether I remember the video footage of the taped Christmas visit I've watched dozens of times, the one in which my grandfather seems—to borrow my husband's phrase—"elegant and kind." There's that mechanical Santa Claus he gave us who drives a red fire truck that blasts "Jingle Bells" as it crashes repeatedly into the bookcase. There's our graceful, longhaired grey tabby—over twenty years gone—who stalks across the frame. There's the slight West Texas drawl in the way he says my name. I'm afraid they may be memories of the video and not my own. I see myself—an impossible perspective   crouched under the green wire pine.

. . . .

Hans Christian Andersen was so phobic about being buried alive that he kept a note by his bedside: "I only appear to be dead." This way, no one would stick him in a pine box and shovel six feet of dirt on him as he dozed. On his actual deathbed, at age seventy, he begged a close friend to do him a favor: after he died, please slash his veins, to make sure he wouldn't wake up, alive, confined in a dark, airless coffin. Perhaps I visited the Museum of Death because of a similar sort of horror. Or maybe I remain furious at the museum's subject. But what can I do with the severed head of the Bluebeard of Paris except stare? Or with lockets and pins stuffed with the hair of Victorians? What stories can these taxidermied albinos tell through their impossible tableau?

Bluebeard's wife Fatima remains silent after discovering his murderous secret. She says nothing at the party to her friends about what she's seen in the forbidden chamber. Couldn't someone have helped her? Why did she accept her fate and try to hide the key? My mother remained silent about her suspicions at the

Christmas party she attended with her parents and my father in the early seventies. As she looked around the room, she realized every guest—save the ones in her party—was gay. She studied her father's gestures as he stood next to Jim, Leslie playing piano, the many members of the local community theater group talking animatedly and clinking their drinks. Maybe he felt he didn't need to say anything. Maybe he felt that cross the Ku Klux Klan once burned in his front yard in Jackson had said enough. Maybe he believed the truth would damage our family.

I'm glad my mother shares with me her stories, especially the dark or surprising ones. They help me better understand my family, including the members whose lives overlapped only briefly— five years, seven years—with my own. I'm glad she was voted resident storyteller in her college social club. Since I can remember she's been my resident storyteller, too. There isn't an anecdote out there too terrifying or gruesome or scandalous. They're our *Tales of Mother Goose*. There isn't a forbidden door in the castle that she won't unlock. *Father Hanes's Daughter*. There's a Bluebeard—or two—shifting shapes in the story, a grandfather who died, a tattoo artist hiding bodies in the secret chamber. Like the clever daughter in "Fitcher's Bird," I'd find those limbs, arrange them, and watch the fragments begin to resurrect and walk.